MORE MEMORIES OF
DONCASTER

The publishers would like to thank the following companies for their

support in the production of this book

G W Askew Printers Ltd

C Barnsdale & Son

Cooplands

Doncaster College

Doncaster Racecourse

Grantham Brundel & Farran

Graziano Trasmissioni CH Ltd

Ice-Cream Direct

Jeld-Wen UK Ltd

Lewis Homes (Yorkshire) Limited

PTE Plant

Smith Bros (Caer Conan) Wholesale Ltd

Walkers Nursery

Yorkshire Caravans

First published in Great Britain by True North Books Limited
Garden Street North
Halifax
West Yorkshire
HX3 6AE
01422 344344

ISBN 1 903204 75 5

Text, design and origination by True North Books Limited
Printed and bound by The Amadeus Press Limited

MORE MEMORIES OF
DONCASTER

Loaned to DLIS by Dawn White

Contents

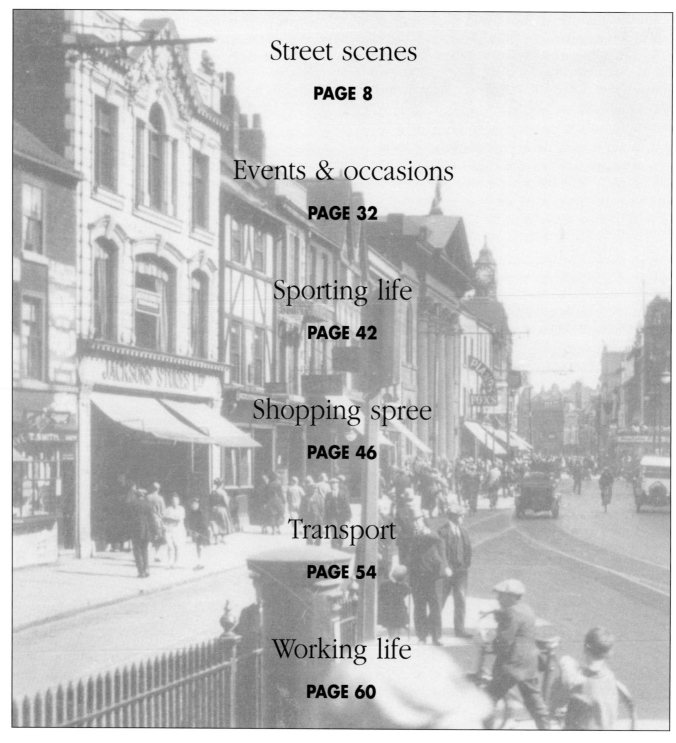

Introduction

History is bunk. Those words of Henry Ford, uttered in 1919 when he was in the witness box suing the Chicago Tribune, show that the great motor car mogul knew a lot about automobiles, but little about what is important in life. Our personal and national histories are the making of us, defining the sort of people we are today. Of particular reference are the experiences to which we can directly relate: the times through which we have lived and the influences that our parents and grandparents brought to bear upon us. However, as the years roll by and we get that little longer in the tooth, the memory begins to play a few tricks. Images become clouded and the edges become blurred. Questions are asked about the past from which our modern culture has developed and, if the truth be told, the answers that are given contain an element of guesswork about how life used to be. Fortunately, the camera is a boon to jogging the memory and assisting us in coming to accurate conclusions about the lifestyle of the 20th century. For anyone interested in looking back over the years that contributed to our current way of life in this town, a book such as 'More Memories of

Doncaster' provides the ideal aide-memoire. Yet, it is not just a publication for the grey haired and wrinkly amongst us, for the younger generation can take just as much pleasure in turning over the pages of modern history and reliving the days when dad was a Teddy boy or gran a member of the Land Army.

'More Memories of Doncaster' is not intended to be a dry and dusty retelling of events of the last century, but a celebration of the middle years of those days that are somehow sandwiched in black and white, somewhere between sepia and colour. They are the times for which nostalgia rules supreme, because we can almost reach out and touch them. Even if we cannot quite remember our town as it once was, at least our families have told us about the lifestyle and architecture of those days and the activities that brought us fun and fulfilment. This book contains delightful images that have been plucked from the past, accompanied by carefully crafted captions that are intended to be both informative and provocative. Hopefully, they will produce as much argument about the merits of the times described as they do agreement of opinion. But, the main

purpose of 'More Memories of Doncaster' is to allow the reader to enjoy a nostalgic glow when contemplating the development from cloche hats and flat caps of the 1920s to the hot pants and flares of the 1970s. We will move from an age of terraced housing to high rise flats and from the tram to pedestrianised streets.

But life did not just begin in the 1900s. Doncaster has its own particular history that stretches far back before the 20th century. This South Yorkshire town and metropolitan area, now occupying 225 square miles of the county, has its historic heart on the River Don on the site of a Roman military station that was named Danum. By adding 'caster', the Roman name for a fort, to this the root for the modern name for our town can easily be determined. After the legions departed the Saxons settled here and Doncaster came under the influence of the kings of Northumbria. It is thought that the 7th century King Edwin provided the inspiration for St Mary Magdalene's, one of the first Christian churches to built on his lands, in the spot that is now Market Place. After William the Conqueror defeated Harold II at the Battle of Hastings the Normans held sway. They built Conisbrough Castle, the edifice that still has one of the best surviving circular castle keeps in all of Europe. It takes its name from the Anglo-Saxon 'Cyninges-burh' or 'defended area of the king'. The manor of Conisbrough had been held by Harold and the title passed to William's son in law, William, Earl Warenne after the Conquest. In the Middle Ages Doncaster grew as the market town of a rich agricultural district. Its first royal charter was granted in 1194 by Richard the Lionheart. This gave Doncaster people the right to pay their annual taxes directly to the Exchequer instead of the King's agent. This was the first of 14 royal charters that were given to the town over the years until the 1836 decree by William IV that related to the continuation of the quarter sessions courts.

Many of the intervening charters referred to fairs and markets, as befitted a town that relied heavily on its surrounding agricultural lands and its own standing as an important market town. Doncaster was also a major point on the stagecoach routes and a flourishing horse-breeding trade developed, inspiring the growth of horse racing that had begun on Town Moor as early as 1600. The world's oldest classic race, the St Leger, was first held in Doncaster in 1776, though not using that name until two years later, and continues to be a major attraction today.

Loaned to DLIS by Dawn White

Also dating from that century, the 1749 Mansion House, the former official residence of the Mayor, is one of only three such houses in the whole of Britain.

The influence of the industrial revolution, in the late 18th and 19th centuries, changed the face of Doncaster forever. The focus shifted from rural life to that dominated by coal and the heavier industries, particularly after the arrival of the railway in 1849. The large locomotive works that went on to produce such magnificent beasts as Flying Scotsman and Mallard also helped swell the town's population by the increase in its industrial workforce. During the first half of the last century Doncaster was an important player in glass, iron, munitions and fossil fuels, but as these industries declined so its focus shifted. It has grown as the leisure and service centre for the new mining communities and has acquired many new industries while retaining importance as an agricultural market. The town's population is now about 80,000, but the wider district is somewhere in the region of 289,000.

It is now to that changing face of the town that 'More Memories of Doncaster' takes us. It is time for the reader to delve into a world when Frenchgate was a street throbbing with activity, as cars and pedestrians dodged one another on their way towards Trafford Street. This was long before ring roads and shopping malls were created. Look again with a nostalgic eye at the cinemas where courting couples enjoyed a fond embrace on the back row as spoilsport usherettes played the beams from their torches towards them. Jive in the dancehall to Danny and the Juniors' 'At the Hop' or enjoy the last waltz as the strains of Mantovani's 'Moulin Rouge' set the correct romantic atmosphere. We are going back in time to an era when men gave up their seats on the bus for a lady without being sneered at for being sexist. There really was a moment in history when you could smile at a young woman in the street and say 'Hello' without being accused of harassment. Children bought two ounces of sherbet lemons and penny Arrow bars and cloth was sold by the yard, not the metre. Men drank from glasses, not directly from the bottle, and women enjoyed a sweet sherry rather than a pint of lager. Grass was something that you mowed on a Sunday afternoon instead of smoking secretively and footballers with Brylcreemed hair played at centre forward and not as pony-tailed strikers. Bunk, Mr Ford? Sheer, unbridled nostalgia, dear Henry.

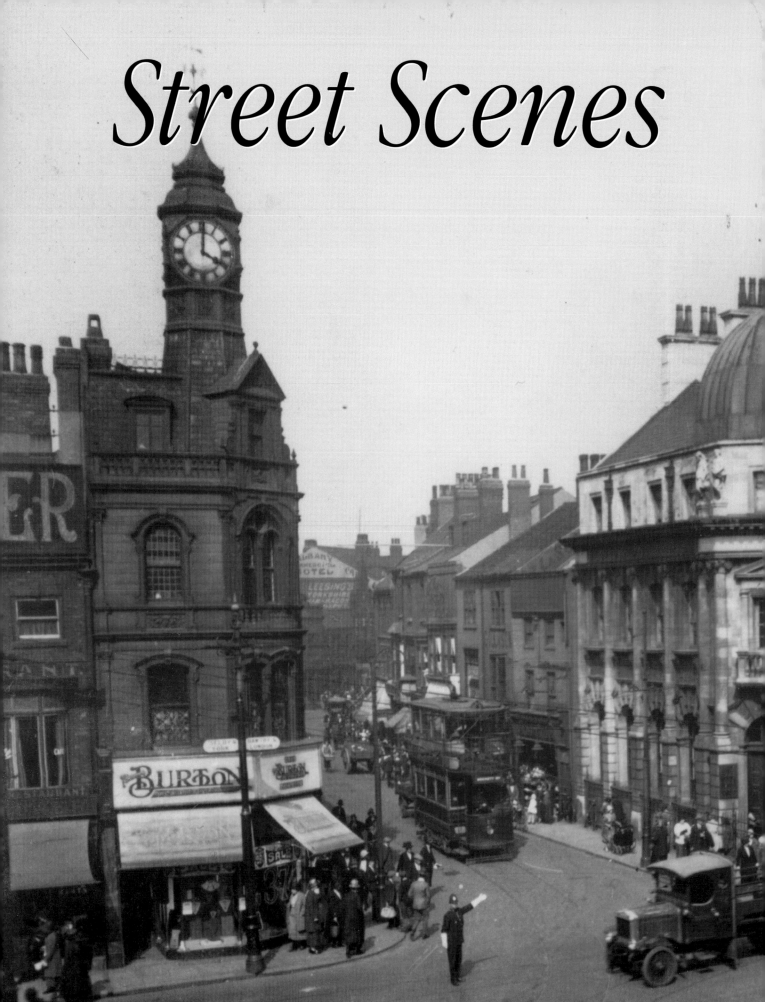

Street Scenes

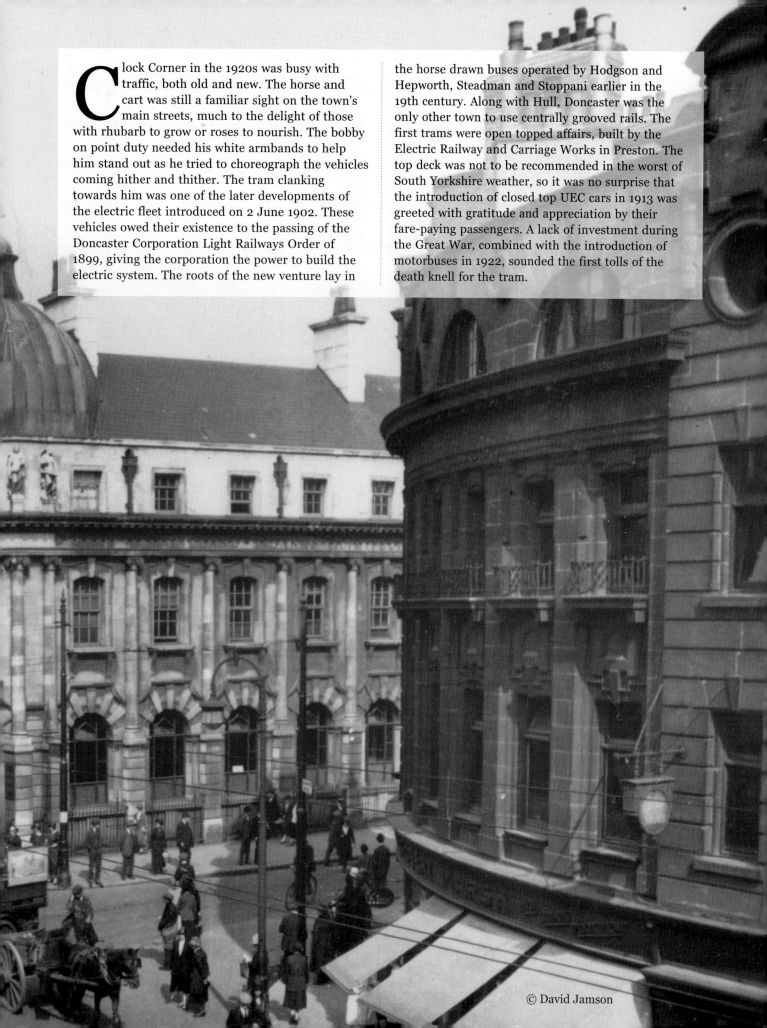

Clock Corner in the 1920s was busy with traffic, both old and new. The horse and cart was still a familiar sight on the town's main streets, much to the delight of those with rhubarb to grow or roses to nourish. The bobby on point duty needed his white armbands to help him stand out as he tried to choreograph the vehicles coming hither and thither. The tram clanking towards him was one of the later developments of the electric fleet introduced on 2 June 1902. These vehicles owed their existence to the passing of the Doncaster Corporation Light Railways Order of 1899, giving the corporation the power to build the electric system. The roots of the new venture lay in the horse drawn buses operated by Hodgson and Hepworth, Steadman and Stoppani earlier in the 19th century. Along with Hull, Doncaster was the only other town to use centrally grooved rails. The first trams were open topped affairs, built by the Electric Railway and Carriage Works in Preston. The top deck was not to be recommended in the worst of South Yorkshire weather, so it was no surprise that the introduction of closed top UEC cars in 1913 was greeted with gratitude and appreciation by their fare-paying passengers. A lack of investment during the Great War, combined with the introduction of motorbuses in 1922, sounded the first tolls of the death knell for the tram.

Frenchgate pre 1931 was its usual hustling, bustling self. Notice how little boys in those days dressed as smaller versions of their fathers. Each wore a similar flat cap and jacket as if a clone of dear old dad. Jackson's Stores did not survive the Churchway/North Bridge remodelling in later years, but Fox's Music, further down on the same side, is still trading. Founded in Burnley by Charles J Fox, the Frenchgate shop was opened in 1924. There are now a number of branches in other towns and cities, including Sheffield, Nottingham, Leeds, Barnsley, Lincoln and Hull. In addition to outlets in the Frenchgate Centre and on Nether Hall Road, there is a small one in the Waterdale Centre, close to Doncaster Central Library. This one promotes itself as a purveyor of keyboards and guitars, a true reflection

of how tastes in music have changed since the prewar years. This shop presents a bright face in its presentation and is something of an oasis in a slightly grubby centre lacking any semblance of beauty. A small knot of men gathered on the pavement to the right were probably waiting for opening time and a pint of Bass at the Bay Horse. Dating from 1828, this pub had been rebuilt in 1909. It was to close in 1966. The adjacent

Electra was the town's first purpose built picture house. It was altered in 1931 and renamed 'Regal' to take advantage of the new interest in talking movies. On the day of this photograph the main feature was a lighthearted comedy about a racehorse owner, directed by Frank Capra, and would be remade in 1950 as 'Riding High', featuring the old groaner, Bing Crosby.

Gentlemen's outfitters prided themselves in providing the finest of tailoring at keen prices. Names such as Alexandre, Hepworth and the Fifty Shilling Tailor were common names on Britain's High streets. Some had particular slogans to help customers remember their names. John Collier was 'the window to watch' and Burton 'the tailor of taste'. This latter enterprise, founded by Montague Burton, born Meshe Minsky in Lithuania, soon expanded from its small base in Chesterfield to a huge factory in Leeds. In the 1920s and 1930s Burton was opening a new shop in a different town every month. The chain had a prestigious retail outlet at Clock Corner, as seen in this 1940s view. The widening of Baxtergate in the early 1890s made room for the building of the York City and County Banking Company Building on the right. It was erected in 1897 at a cost of £10,000. Later in the next century the Midland Bank took over the premises, to be followed by the HSBC. Baxtergate takes its name from the obsolete term for a baker. It is possible that a guild of bakers or baxters once flourished near here. The name of the street goes back to 1556 when Bloody Mary Tudor was our monarch. The cars and the trolleybuses have long been banished from this part of town. Shoppers can enjoy a safe haven from the traffic as they walk the pedestrianised area underneath the bank's green dome and imposing pillars that lend a sense of grandeur to Doncaster's commercial heart.

It was race day and the crowds surged past the Guildhall as they crowded Frenchgate on their way to the Racecourse in September 1927. Regular meetings were held as long ago as the early 1600s. The town's legislators, with a whiff of Puritanism, became concerned about the unruly and unsavoury elements who took advantage of the occasion to engage in pickpocketing and brawling. In June 1615 a decision was taken to stop racing, but perhaps fearful of a public backlash, the intention was never put into practice. The races only became properly organised at the start of the following century when a confederation of 'gentle-folk', as they described themselves, took matters in hand. Gradually, the town fathers came round and gave the sport their blessing. In 1766 the Doncaster Gold Cup was instituted. It was about that time that Lord Rockingham met with a group of wealthy friends including Lt. Col. Anthony St Leger for a dinner at the Red Lion Inn. Many believe that this gathering was the inspiration behind the running of the first St Leger, named after the colonel who was a local resident and went on to become the governor of St Lucia. How many of those streaming down towards South Parade and Bennetthorpe would lose their shirts is hard to say, but it is a safe bet that they had an enjoyable day roaring themselves hoarse, if you do not mind the pun.

Some confusion exists about the naming of Frenchgate. It may have come to gain its title because of the connections with the Normans, but others insist that it reflects links with Franciscan monks. However, they are not thought to have come to Doncaster until 1307, some 30 years after it was referred to as 'Vicus Franciscus'. Whatever the true origins, there is no doubt that Frenchgate has had an important part to play in the daily life of the town. This scene here is c1930 as both tram tracks and a trolleybus heading off towards Clock Corner can be seen. The Guildhall, with its impressive columned frontage, lay in between such shops as Tom Smith's and Brough's on the left and Fox's Music further down. The Guildhall, built in 1848, housed the old law courts and police headquarters. The pediment was surmounted by the very appropriate figure of 'Justice', salvaged from the old Town Hall on Market Place. It was a sorry day for lovers of classically styled architecture when the building was pulled down. The locals going about their business demonstrated the accepted norms of dress for the times. Women wore hats that had brims that extended down in front of their foreheads and almost over their eyes. Most men wore the ubiquitous large, flat cap, though some of the more middle class favoured homburgs.

Above: A 'laughing mirthquake' was the way the cinema poster advertised this week's feature film. Situated at what later became known as Gaumont Corner, the Majestic was screening a version of the Victorian farce written for the stage by Brandon Thomas. The complicated plot revolved around an undergraduate having to impersonate his friend's rich aunt. She was from Brazil - where the nuts come from. The mayor, Councillor S Morris, opened the cinema in December 1920 as the South Parade Cinema. An orchestra conducted by Walter Hindle provided additional entertainment for patrons filling the 1,800 seats. Renamed the Majestic in 1922, cinemagoers packed the auditorium to follow the adventures of heartthrob Rudolph Valentino in such epic silent movies as 'The Sheikh' and 'Blood and Sand'. Women wept uncontrollably when he died from a ruptured appendix in 1926. The Majestic was demolished in 1933, reopening as the Gaumont on 3 September 1934 with the musical 'Evergreen', starring Jessie Matthews. She had a long acting career that included 'Mrs Dale's Diary', the popular postwar radio soap opera. On that opening night Hebron Morland played the Wonder Compton Organ. Audiences of the day felt cheated if they did not have a full night's entertainment and it was common to have live music, two films, a newsreel and several shorts for the price of a single ticket. On 8 April 1973 the Gaumont was converted into a three screen cinema. It was renamed the Odeon on 20 January 1987, but had no connection with the former Ritz and other Odeon that had been on Hallgate.

Far right: Even in 1937 signs on the pavement were offering advice or instruction to motorists. 'No waiting' is not confined to the second half of the century and some parts of town, such as Frenchgate, had their restrictions in force. The pedestrian crossing outside Greaves' furnishers was a recent innovation and, elsewhere, electrically controlled traffic lights had only been in place for a few years. Looking across the junction with Trafford Street towards North Bridge, many of the buildings on the left would disappear as the Northern Bus Station, Trades and Labour Club and inner relief road were created. The flag fluttering outside Greaves' store might have been there to celebrate George VI's coronation or as a reminder that this company prided itself on its patriotism. In the distance, a gable end proudly proclaimed the virtue of Taddy Ales, brewed in Tadcaster by Samuel Smith: its Old Brewery was founded in 1758 and still produces such fine ales as Nut Brown and Oatmeal today, in conjunction with its traditional bitter. There are not many small, independent brewers left nowadays, so it is good to see that Yorkshire's oldest brewery is still going strong. Donny drinkers in 1937 would be horrified if they knew that traditional beers with their hoppy tastes were to be replaced in the 1960s by pressurised, 'watery rubbish' like Watney's Red Barrel.

ooking from the Reindeer Hotel on Hallgate, across the Silver Street and Cleveland Street junction into High Street, the cabinet making and furnishing store of Sheard, Binnington and Company can just be seen. The firm was jointly set up by Henry Binnington and George Sheard and flourished during the period 1885-1953. The trolleybus is passing one of Doncaster's most famous hotels. Until 1909, this was the Ram, but we all know it today as the Danum. Under its distinctive dome, unhappily missed by the photographer, 50 bedrooms, bathrooms and a garage provided comfortable service for visitors to the town or travellers stopping off on

their way along the old Great North Road. Danum is the old Roman name for the Don and the one given to the fort the invaders constructed in AD71. Trolley-buses were extensively used in Doncaster earlier than in most other towns. Powers were obtained in 1926 to run them on existing tram routes, though it was not until 19 August 1928 that the first such vehicles made the journey north to Bentley. The initial fleet of 10 buses included Garrett and Karrier double deckers, with the latter make dominating the order books in the 1930s as the service expanded. The fleet was based in a depot on Greyfriars Road that had formerly been used by trams.

Above: A night out at the pictures in 1936 was a weekly must for every courting couple in the town. It was an opportunity to be alone with a sweetheart, away from the prying eyes of mum and dad. A cuddle on the back row and a box of Payne's Poppets on her lap and a girl could almost be persuaded that her beau had something of the Douglas Fairbanks Jr about him, if it were not for the spot on his chin. Going to the Gaumont Palace was good value for money as there were great films around. There was suspense in 'The Petrified Forest', with Bette Davis, Leslie Howard and Humphrey Bogart, or adventure and thrills in 'The Charge of the Light Brigade', starring Errol Flynn and Olivia de Haviland. The rolling programme of entertainment led to a quaint style of viewing for many in the audience. It was common for people to enter the cinema halfway through a film, watch the middle and the end, followed by the remainder of the offerings. They stayed in their seats as the show was repeated and watched the beginning of the story they had missed a couple of hours earlier. When the evening was over, the boy walked the girl home and gave her a goodnight peck on the cheek at the end of the street. It was no good waiting until the front gate as her father was watching from the window just in case she was not back by 10.30 at the latest.

Below: Peake's piano and organ shop on Hallgate also did a good trade in sheet music. Although many families owned wind up gramophones on which to play their Tommy Dorsey or Gracie Fields records, making your own music was a popular, alternative source of home entertainment in the 1930s and 1940s. There was often a piano in the parlour on which to tinkle out the hit tunes of the day. The sale of sheet music determined the first popular music charts to be published in Britain and it was not until late 1952 that the first hit parade for records was compiled. The beacons on the striped poles near the Ritz cinema were the brainchild of the Ministry of Transport, led from 1934-37 by Leslie Hore-Belisha (1893-1957). After this stint concerning himself with our roads, he went on to act as minister for war until 1940. During the mid 1930s a whole raft of road safety measures was introduced. Accident statistics and the number of fatalities were among the worst in Europe and out of all proportion to the number of cars on the road. Anyone could get behind the wheel of a car until the driving test was at last instituted. The use of dipped headlights outside built up areas was made compulsory and 30 mph speed limits in towns imposed in 1935. Belisha beacons were placed at strategic spots of heavy pedestrian use, but education of the public to use the crossings safely took a while to have effect. Initially, studs marked the crossing path. It was not until 1951 that the black and white markings that earned the nickname 'zebra crossing' were introduced.

We seldom see motor cycle combinations these days, but they were a common sight either side of the last war. Here, two of them are making their way along Frenchgate towards High Street. Older motorists and members of motoring organisations will recall the days when the AA and RAC patrolmen, riding their bikes and sidecars, would salute a member displaying the appropriate badge as he drove past. This form of transport was quite economical as petrol consumption was low and a man could take his family out for a spin with his good lady clutching his waist and the two children squashed in beside them. They were rather draughty and not too pleasant an experience in wet weather, but needs must when money was tight. Only when family saloon cars, such as the Ford Popular, became affordable in the 1950s did the motorbike and sidecar largely become a thing of the past. The machine closer to the camera was passing the Guildhall. Its lovely columns and imposing presence, dating from 1848, were tragically lost to the town when so-called progress had its way and the building was demolished. The answer to the question as to why its façade could not have been incorporated into the new Marks and Spencer development has never been properly given. Was it too much to ask that a piece of architectural beauty and historic value could have been preserved?

Loaned to DLIS by Ralph Mann

town from Heinkel 1-11s and Junker 52s. This was a salutary warning for the sort of war we could expect if Mr Chamberlain could not get some form of agreement with Herr Hitler when he visited Munich the following year. Winston Churchill had been advising the country that we needed to build up our armed forces and defence resources. Future events would prove the wisdom of his words.

Top: Cleveland Street was named for the Duke of Cleveland and opened as a thoroughfare in 1834. William Henry Vane became a Marquis in 1827 before rising to the dukedom in 1833. The Cleveland and Vane names have some interesting history. Sir Henry Vane and his son, also Henry, were prominent politicians in the 17th century. The elder served Charles I as his secretary of state and was canny enough to be able to serve in Cromwell's government as well. The younger Henry, an avowed Puritan, became leader of the House of Commons: Charles II had him executed after the Restoration. At about this time Barbara Villiers, Duchess of Cleveland, was currying favour with the merry monarch and reputedly bore him several children, but we had better gloss over this matter in the interests of decency! Cleveland Street, at its corner with Baker Street, has seen many changes as it was remodelled in the interests of highway and relief road improvements. Houses and old roads disappeared under the developer's demolition ball. There was once a lovely shop here, as indicated by the sign for Stamp Corner. Some readers may recall the times they had here or at their local newsagents, buying a sixpenny packet of mixed stamps from countries across the globe. How colourful and exotic some of them were. We had hours of fun swapping them with our pals at school and sticking them with adhesive hinges into huge albums.

Left: On the corner of Frenchgate and Trafford Street T Greaves and Company celebrated that it was an English firm of furnishers. Just to emphasise the point, a Union flag flew boldly from the pole above the shop next to the Danum café. Would Greaves be allowed to advertise his ethnicity in such a brazen way today in this politically correct world of ours? There was even a case in the Dales a year or two ago when someone was threatened with prosecution for flying the white rose of Yorkshire above his farmhouse. Back in 1937, just as the first Belisha beacons blinked on the footpath, there was little chance of anyone being thought offensive for declaring his nationality. Quite the opposite, in fact, as across Europe the stormclouds of war were gathering. The Spaniards were conducting a bitter civil conflict, with Franco's fascist forces receiving support from the Condor squadrons of Germany's Luftwaffe pilots. Guernica, the cultural and spiritual home of the Basques, was destroyed by bombs unleashed on the

Below: Sandwiched between Taylor and Sons and the cleaners, Clarks of Retford, the solid face of banking was offered by the chunky look of the York County Savings Bank. Inside here were tellers and counter staff who knew their customers. The manager worked behind the scenes, but knew the value of everyone's worth from the figures he scrutinised carefully. His position was something akin to that of a headmaster. When a customer received a request to come into the bank to discuss his account, then he knew trouble was brewing in the same way a naughty child dreaded the summons to the head's office. Such personal contact, whether enjoyable or otherwise, has been lost to the financial world for some time. Branches in villages and small towns have closed in the interests of efficiency. It might be better for the banks, but what about the clients? It is our money, after all. Can any reader put a hand on heart and say that he really knows the name of his local bank manager. It is more than likely that account holders are so busy trying to get some sense out of a call centre in Dublin or Delhi that they have no opportunity to deal with real people in the know.

Right: This jolly little baby Austin was a well loved runabout, popular in the late 50s and early 60s. If it could speak it might have said something rude to the garage on Bennetthorpe that it had just passed. That was the main Ford dealership in Doncaster, with a prime position on the old Great North Road. Edgar Charlesworth, with assistance from his father, George, first traded in 1913 in Wombwell, next to the Earl of Doncaster Arms and had been Ford dealers since 1920. They established the company in these premises in 1926 and soon E and G Charlesworth's dealership had gained a reputation for excellent service. The firm's standing in the motoring world led to recognition from the authorities during World War II. The firm's mechanics were given the responsible task of refitting and repairing military vehicles required

for the war effort. During the boom years in motoring in the 1950s, when car ownership escalated at a dizzy rate, Charlesworth's was kept very busy as new Populars, Prefects, Consuls, Anglias and Zephyrs rolled off the production lines. The ownership of the company remains in family hands, though it moved to Barnby Dun in the 1990s. George died in 1954 at the ripe old age of 83, but his son was still going strong at the time of this photograph. However, Edgar joined his father in that great garage in the sky in 1964.

Now what do you think has caught the eye of this young cyclist on Cleveland Street? You must have forgotten your childhood if you think he has even noticed the bargains in cloth inside Harry Clarke's drapery. He is certainly too young to take any interest in the coffin nails being sold as Woodbines or Park Drive at the tobacconist, though his big brother might be tempted to buy a packet of five or even a single fag if the shopkeeper can be persuaded to split a carton. This boy's gaze is clearly focused on the model shop in between. People of any age, but young at heart, took delight in the establishment run by David and Michael Cuttriss. Airfix kits to put together imitation Spitfires, model railways with replicas of the great steam locomotives of the 1930s,

Dinky cars and all manner of balsa, glue and tissue were on sale here. Enthusiasts, who had bedrooms given over to transformers powering tracks criss-crossing the floor, were able to get bits of sponge to make bushes for the hillside they had made from papier-mâché or small figures to place on the railway platform. Elsewhere in the house, mum had to duck to avoid being decapitated by a little De Haviland Comet strung from the boxroom ceiling or move carefully past a miniature steam engine fuelled by methylated spirit. The brothers started their business a few years before the war, eventually moving from the Cleveland Street site to Duke Street in the mid 1960s. When they retired in 1983 the business went with them, along with a host of childhood memories.

Loaned to DLIS by Geoff Elvin

Above: The first motorbus route, using Bristol vehicles was inaugurated in October 1922 on the route to Skellow, with services to Rossington, Hatfield and Edlington following shortly afterwards. The Corporation was slow to develop the deployment of these vehicles, favouring trolleybuses as a more economical option. It was only after their phasing out in the early 1960s, partly attributable to the building of new roads, that the motorbus became the flagship of public transport. Even then, many of the buses still used former trolley bodies relocated on new chassis. Doncaster Corporation Transport ceased to exist on 1 April 1974 when, under local government reorganisation, the South Yorkshire Passenger Transport Executive was formed. This pair of buses on Cleveland Street comprises a Daimler CV6 (Tar Burner) and an AEC Regent. They are outside the newly opened Thrift supermarket, one of the early entrants in this new style of retailing that changed our shopping patterns in the 1960s. Quite why we were so taken with the idea of serving ourselves, instead of getting the grocer to fill our bags for us or have his lad pedal an order box round to the house, is only understandable when realising the time that was saved. We no longer had to go from shop to shop as the supermarket provided a variety, sufficient to our needs. We did miss the chinwag, though.

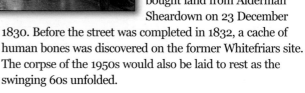

Below: In 1960 there was 'a wind of change' in the air, as British Prime Minister Macmillan told the South African government in a speech in Capetown. He was referring to that country's racial policies, but there was also a turn towards a new order elsewhere. In America, the country saw the former World War II veteran Dwight Eisenhower complete two terms of office and decided that a different, forward looking breed was needed to lead it into the 60s. The USA turned to a Catholic radical in John F Kennedy, the youngest man to enter the White House, and at home we began to question the policies of the establishment. Supermac, as cartoonists dubbed the British leader, was not getting any younger and the Tory party made the mistake of choosing the aristocratic Alec Douglas-Home to replace the ailing Macmillan in 1963. He only lasted a year before being swept from power. This sedate scene was photographed on Priory Place, a street that had also provided a home for the Town Clerk and Borough Engineer. The drab, grey atmosphere surrounding the Volvo B18 and Hillman Minx De Luxe would be transformed into a vibrant and colourful one of mini-skirted girls and long haired lads chattering away about a man on the moon and Concorde in the sky as the decade ended. Priory Place was created after the Corporation bought land from Alderman Sheardown on 23 December 1830. Before the street was completed in 1832, a cache of human bones was discovered on the former Whitefriars site. The corpse of the 1950s would also be laid to rest as the swinging 60s unfolded.

Heading towards the Famous Army Stores on Hallgate, probably in the late 1950s, the woman leading the way was getting some looks for her choice of fashion. To see a young lady out and about in trousers was an unfamiliar sight. The man could be from almost any postwar era since topcoats and trousers have only seen marginal changes. Perhaps the favoured length of raincoat and width of trouser leg or turn-up has shifted from time to time, but the basics have remained the same. Not so for the fairer sex. In the late 1940s, Christian Dior introduced the New Look, with its concentration on the ultra feminine 'figure of eight' shape, handspan waists and soft shoulders. The next decade had women reaching for full, billowing skirts over starched petticoats as they tottered along on stiletto heels. The swinging 60s offered mini skirts as hemlines rose, as did male blood pressure at the sight. We then came to hot pants, maxi dresses and trouser suits. What fun it was being a girl, but it cost a few bob to keep up with fashion trends. Money was a secondary consideration as no one with a spark about her wanted to wear sensible shoes and practical skirts. There would be time enough for that when they got old, such as thirty-something.

Right: Two of the most famous names in British 20th century heritage and culture appear in this 1965 scene on Frenchgate. Boot's chemist's shop and the Morris Minor are about as typically Brit as you can get. Although the name of Jesse Boot (1850-1931) is well known to most people, it was his father, John Boot, who founded the company in a small shop in Nottingham selling herbal remedies. He died in 1860 and his widow ran the business on her own until her son joined her after leaving school at 13. In 1871 they became partners as Mary and Jesse Boot - Herbalists, not becoming Boot and Company until 1883. The following year the first shop outside Nottingham was opened, thus preparing the way for establishing the company name on High streets across the country. By the start of World War I, Boot's had over 500 shops in business. Jesse Boot was knighted in 1909 and became Lord Trent in 1928. He never drove a Morris Minor as the first model designed by Alec Issigonis (1906-88) did not take to the road until 1948. A reliable car with excellent steering and cornering qualities, it was the first all British car to sell a million and remained in production until 1971. Issigonis was also responsible for the BMC Mini and was knighted in 1969 for his services to the automobile industry.

© Gordon Evans

Right: H Samuel trades from this location today. In the 1950s the main retail premises at Clock Corner were occupied by Burton's, 'the tailor of taste', but by 1965 cheap and cheerful jewellery was sold on this site. Ratner's had taken over the ground floor, under the room where men once used to practise their skills on the green baize of the billiard table, dreaming of becoming another Joe Davis or Horace Lindrum. Wagers would be struck as men sought to hustle their way to a few extra shillings to pad out their wage packets by indulging in a pastime that the straightlaced referred to as being the sign of a misspent youth. Even the most inveterate gambler would have been hard pressed to back Gerald Ratner, a member of the family firm who rather let the side down with a throwaway remark in 1991 when he referred to his firm's products as total junk. He actually used a ruder four letter word and £500 million was suddenly wiped from the value of

© Gordon Evans

Ratner stock. The 'jewellers of repute' were not best pleased. Not surprisingly Mr Ratner left the business the following year and was last heard of running a gymnasium in Henley and dallying with the idea of relaunching his jewellery interests on the internet. He is not the only businessman to have suffered from foot in mouth disease as the Royal Bank of Scotland deputy chairman discovered in 2003 when he described a £750,000 bonus as 'not enough to buy bragging power in a Soho wine bar'.

Below: This elevated 1960s'photograph has us looking down towards the bus station, Waterdale and St James' Street in the foreground. In the early 19th century it was an area for horse sales. The famous Tattersall's held horse sales at Glasgow Paddocks until 1957. The Waterdale district stretched from St James' Baths to the Chequer Road roundabout and was mentioned as

'Weterdale' in a 1535 deed. It was largely fields and open spaces until Henry Preston built Beechfield House on Waterdale Close and, gradually, houses and connecting streets began to appear. The area was part of the redevelopment programme begun not long after this picture was taken. High rise flats appeared and Waterdale was subjected to the Golden Acres project that spawned the ugly face of the shopping centre that included maisonettes and flats on parts of its upper storeys. Established traders and residents were forced to relocate as a result of the redevelopment work. Trafford Way, part of the inner relief road, now separates St James' Street from Waterdale. The brewery advert, bottom right, refers to the ales produced in Newark by Richard Warwick. His company acquired the Trent Brewery, run by Joseph Richardson, in 1889. The two men joined forces and the firm was restyled as Warwicks and Richardsons Ltd.

Centre: Redevelopment was well under way around the junction of St Sepulchre Gate and Cleveland Street on 6 July 1962. It was on this day that the Australian Rod Laver confirmed his prowess as the world's top amateur tennis player when he won Wimbledon for the second year in succession, blitzing his fellow countryman, Marty Mulligan, for the loss of just six games. Laver, or the 'Rockhampton Rocket' as he was nicknamed, swept opponents aside with the ruthlessness of the bulldozers altering the face of Doncaster. In the background, the high rise St James' flats were beginning to take shape. Town planners across Britain saw this form of housing as the cure to the nation's future needs. Communities, happy in terraced houses on streets where they could socialise and be neighbourly, were put one on top of another with little in the way of recreational space. In many cases, this type of building took away a sense of corporate belonging and became the catalyst for social problems and loutish behaviour. The YMCA logo on the building on the left is of one of those that now conjures up silly thoughts of the Village People pop group and people doing a daft dance to the 70s disco tune. Similarly, in earlier days many could not hear Rossini's 'William Tell Overture' without conjuring up a vision of the Lone Ranger riding off into the sunset on Silver. Doncaster's first purpose built hospital formerly occupied this building. It was demolished in 1963.

Bottom: At the start of the 1960s, as the late Adam Faith warbled 'Poor Me' to the top of the charts, the song's composer, Les Vandyke, might have been inspired by the thoughts of this van driver. The local fruit and potato merchant was not having much joy in negotiating an entry into the traffic pouring down from North Bridge. The bumper to bumper queue, not helped by the clutch of buses near the terminus, moved at a snail's pace into town. The congestion on our roads meant that something had to be done to relieve a major headache. The Corporation originally intended to build flyovers at the end of Trafford Street, near where it connected with Frenchgate, and at the junction with Cleveland Street. However, these plans were put into cold storage and the roundabouts and carriageway of the inner relief road begun instead. Bulldozers moved in to flatten a number of the buildings in the area and the face of this part of town changed for evermore. Chapels, pubs, clubs and shops disappeared in the name of progress. Neither was Ye Olde Barrel Restaurant, dating back to Georgian times as the Golden Barrel, spared. Let us hope that the driver of the van belonging to J and JH Peters made it onto Frenchgate before the demolition man's hammer fell. Otherwise, he might be humming Eddie Cochran's 'Three steps to heaven'.

It is February 1965 on Baxtergate, right in the middle of the swinging 60s. Traditional outfitters and shoe shops such as Alexandre and Dolcis are preparing to do battle, in a commercial sense, with the threat posed by the new style of shop that the youngsters love, the boutique. Teens and early twenty-somethings are the new power on the High Streets of our towns. They no longer wish to be young clones of their parents, but are pushing for their own styles and identities. This new breed has something that shopkeepers ignore at their peril, namely money. Most were born as part of the immediate postwar baby boomer years and either do not know or cannot remember the hardship of the austerity years and the days of the ration book. They earn good money and want to spend it as they wish, not as mum and dad dictate. The two elderly gents shuffling along the pavement are probably horrified that the price of a Mary Quant inspired mini skirt is twice what their wives pay for a proper frock with three times the material. But, this is fashion and girls are willing to pay to be part of it. It was in early 1964 that Quant knocked the Paris fashion houses by saying they were out of date. She opened her first boutique, 'Bazaar', in Chelsea and went from strength to strength as Carnaby Street style became the rage.

Events & occasions

The motorcade that swept along Sandford Road, Balby on 11 September 1948 contained two important visitors to Doncaster. King George VI and Queen Elizabeth attracted thousands to line the streets and wave little Union flags as they displayed their support and fondness for the royal couple. This pair had stood firm during the war when lesser beings might have fled the country to take refuge in Canada or some other safe haven. It was an honour to see them in the flesh, even if it might be for just a fleeting moment as the limousine slid by. Sight of the king and queen was largely restricted to newspaper photographs or footage during the Pathé newsreel slot in between feature films at the cinema.

Loaned to DLIS by Dawn White

Homes did not have televisions and so a short glimpse of the real thing was well worth the draughty hours spent waiting on the pavement. Some wellwishers shouted out congratulations to the granny in waiting as her first grandchild, the future Prince Charles, was due in two months' time. Although King George would be dead within four years, his wife lived on into the next century, becoming affectionately remembered in later years as the 'Queen Mum'. While the watchers waited for the procession to arrive, some commented on the news that had come through the previous day: Don Bradman, that Aussie scourge of England bowling, announced his retirement. Needless to say he signed off with a century in his last first class fixture.

Above: Either side of the second world war no major race meeting was complete without a visit from Ras Prince Monolulu (1881-1965). This flamboyant figure, here calling out his famous catchphrase, 'I gotta horse', at Doncaster Racecourse in September 1954, became something of a national character. He even made it onto television on BBC's inaugural broadcasting day on 2 November 1936 when he appeared in the first edition of the magazine series 'Picture Page'. He styled himself as a tipster without equal, but it was his outlandish eccentricity and quick-witted banter that made him popular, rather than the accuracy of his forecasts that he placed in envelopes and sold to punters. Clad in ostrich features, ornate waistcoats and jackets and ballooning trousers, he pretended that he was descended from a remote and historic Ethiopian people. In truth, he was born Peter Carl Mackay and he came from British Guiana, South America. He came to Europe at the turn of the century and worked as a model in Germany, a boxer in France, a fortune-teller in Rome and a fake opera singer in Moscow. On arriving in England, and turning to racing predictions, he was one of a then small group of black immigrants to these shores. He used his charm to counter racism and soon became a well-loved figure, eagerly sought out by cameramen. He died in London's Middlesex Hospital and the racing world mourned a true one-off.

Top left: In September 1925 horse racing dominated the business of the town, even in Market Place. In the background we can make out the blinds belonging to Boddy's wool shop. This branch opened in 1898 and continued to trade from here until 1950. JW Boddy had earlier started business in a shop at 68 St Sepulchre Gate, selling fancy goods. By 1888 he had prospered sufficiently to start a men's outfitters at 60 St Sepulchre Gate. After the closure of the Market Place outlet, the firm returned close to its initial trading position at Nos 63-65. The crowd was not interested in shopping as it had more pressing needs. The tipsters were calling out for attention and people pressed a little closer to see if they could get a bit of inside information about the runners and riders at the day's meeting. Placing a bet was not as straightforward as it is today. Bookmakers' shops were not authorised until the 1960s and street betting was illegal, despite there being any number of bookies' runners who would risk the long arm of the law in swapping betting slips for hard cash. Many men saw a successful flutter as the way to make ends meet. This was a time of low wages and high unemployment that came to a head the following year in the General Strike.

Above: This delightful scene conjures up images of rural England as it appeared in the interwar years. The May Day celebrations evoked symbols of both pagan and Christian rituals as we celebrated Mother Nature and all she brought. Though local practice varied widely, these gatherings commonly included the carrying in procession of trees, green branches or garlands; the appointment of a May King and May Queen and the setting up of a May tree or maypole. Originally such rites were intended to ensure fertility to the crops, and by extension to cattle and human beings, but in most cases this significance was gradually lost. The practices survived merely as popular festivities. A widespread superstition held that washing the face in the May Day morning dew would beautify the skin. Unfortunately, the significance of this day has changed in modern time since politicians hijacked it as a public holiday with left wing overtones. This scene was recorded in the grounds of Conisbrough Castle. The first castle on this site is thought to have been built c1070 and was probably of a motte and bailey design. Hamelin Plantagenet, half-brother of Henry II, converted it to stone in the latter part of the 12th century. He began building in 1174 and completed the keep, surrounded by walls with towers 15 years later. It was one of the first keeps in Britain to be built in a round design. Sir Walter Scott's 1819 historical novel 'Ivanhoe' helped spread Conisbrough's reputation, even if his account of life there in the time of Richard the Lionheart is fictitious.

Below: In a mixture of party frocks, fancy dress and Sunday best these children from Pembroke Avenue, Balby, just off Sandford Road, let it be known that they were celebrating George VI's coronation on 12 May 1937. Paper hats and crowns were worn at jaunty angles on a day originally set aside for the official enthronement of George's elder brother as Edward VIII. The children did not appreciate the turmoil of the latter months of the previous year. Although common knowledge abroad, many Britons were blissfully unaware that the monarchy was facing its biggest crisis for well over a century. For several years the heir to the throne had been conducting an affair with the twice married American socialite Wallis Simpson. When his father, George V, died in early 1936 the new king continued his liaison and scandalised the establishment, particularly the Church of England, by stating his intention to marry Mrs Simpson. Fleet Street did not break the story until early December when the Yorkshire Post reported comments by the Bishop of Bradford about the situation. Controversy raged in the country as people took sides, but the king brought matters to a head when he announced in a radio broadcast on 11 December 1936 that he was abdicating in order to marry. Many said 'Good riddance' to a man who had failed in his duty, but others commiserated with his dilemma. The children in Pembroke Avenue remained unmoved. They were after a good time at their party and achieved their goal noisily.

Right: Six long years of hostilities came to an end in Europe on 7 May 1945, to be followed by the surrender of Japan just over three months later. The relief was unbridled and, particularly on VE Day, crowds spilled out onto the streets. When Winston Churchill broadcast over the loudspeakers in London, the day after the last bullet was fired, the roar of the multitude celebrating victory drowned his voice. Complete

strangers hugged one another and exchanged kisses with people they had never even seen before. Impromptu congas were danced down the road and hokey-cokeys performed around statues in town centres to the accompaniment of blowing whistles and showers of confetti. At Buckingham Palace the royal family appeared on the balcony on eight separate occasions during the day; each time to shouts of 'God save the king!' and loud renditions of 'Rule Britannia'. Every street seemed to be a mirror image of Balby's Surrey Street. Dining tables, church trestles and a right royal mixture of chairs old and new were dragged out into the middle of the road. Flags and bunting, left over from the 1937 Coronation, were pulled out of boxes and flown from lampposts or stretched across the street. Mums in their pinnies used up a week's ration of sugar, eggs, butter and flour to make tasty goodies for the little ones to enjoy in the biggest series of parties the nation has ever seen.

Above right: This loving couple stood proudly outside the front door of the house that was their own perfect little Englishman's castle. Amos and Annie Booker had every reason to be pleased with themselves. Their home at 14 Nelson Street, Hyde Park had won an award for the best decorated property at the time of the coronation of Queen Elizabeth II in the summer of 1953. The clock with which they were presented gained pride of place on the mantelpiece,

Loaned to DLIS by A J Custons

Loaned to DLIS by Kate Pounder

next to the mug and commemorative crown piece that all families collected when we officially welcomed our new monarch after the ceremony at Westminster Abbey. The Bookers spent the whole of their married life in this property. Bringing up seven children in a two bedroomed house was no mean feat, but what the offspring lacked in space was more than made up for by the oceans of love and affection lavished upon them by mum and dad. Christian names often place people in a particular time warp. At some stage in the not too distant future there will be Grandpa Wayne and Grannie Kylie. The Bookers were no exception to the rule. Amos was one of the Biblical names bestowed by Victorian parents and Annie belonged to a series of diminutives like Minnie and Fanny. She predeceased her husband by four years and when Amos passed on, at the ripe old age of 94, it was a blessing that this was before his beloved Nelson Street home was demolished a few months later.

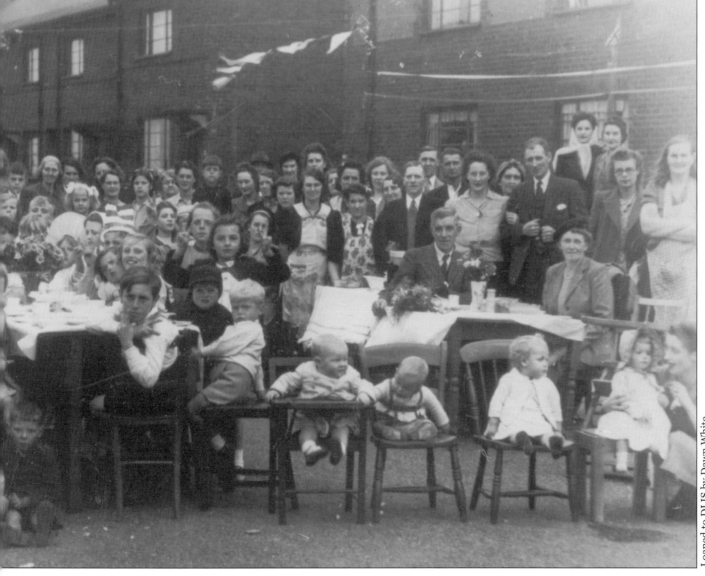

Loaned to DLIS by Dawn White

Below: Just look at those little tots in their pedal cars on Prospect Place. This street is now hemmed in by the triangle of Cleveland Street, Trafford Way and Carr House Road where real cars run along that busy section of Doncaster today. Some 70 years ago children did not have to worry about major traffic problems. They could play in the streets, pretending to drive Alfa Romeos at Brooklands or kick footballs like Dixie Dean, without any worries. Games of 'rally-o' and 'what's the time Mr Wolf?' were enjoyed across the road as hardly anyone in these terraced houses owned a motor vehicle or expected one to come calling. Prospect Place, in keeping with all the nation's streets, had been gaily decorated with streamers, flags and bunting in honour of the silver jubilee of George V. On 6 May 1935 he celebrated the 25th anniversary of his accession to the throne. Such occasions for a monarch are always slightly tempered by sadness as they mark the anniversary of a parent's death, but the king's subjects preferred to concentrate on the joyous aspects of the occasion. Prospect Place used to run from Cemetery Road to Upper Oxford. Much of this property dated from the 1890s and many of the residents relocated to Silverwood House in the 60s and 70s as the area was redeveloped. The north side was demolished to make way for a school, with the remainder being modernised with the assistance of grants from the council.

Loaned to DLIS by E M Walter

Above: 'Vivat Regina!' or words to that effect echoed around Westminster Abbey on 2 June 1953 when the Archbishop of Canterbury, Dr Fisher, lowered the crown onto the head of the 27 year old Elizabeth Alexandra Mary as she started the reign that was to last for over half a century. Her subjects hoped that this would be the dawn of a new Elizabethan age when Britain would reclaim its place as a major and prosperous power, rising from the ashes of two world wars that were being fought within 21 years of each other. Hope was best expressed by the joyous celebrations that took place across the country. Although the day dawned grey and damp, the streets of London were lined by wellwishers who cheered the coronation coaches and were particularly tickled by the appearance of the huge and beaming figure of Queen Salote of Tonga. She waved furiously at the crowd as her carriage filled with water. Away from the capital, parades, dances and parties were held up and down the land. Milton Street even had its own queen to mark the occasion. Here, with her pretty and handsome attendants, she sat regally on her own throne, fashioned from a chair taken from the front parlour. She will be drawing her pension by now, but it is certain that she remembers the thrill of being the centre of attraction and queen for a day.

Bottom: May Day was celebrated in Wadworth by a group of well scrubbed schoolchildren, all having washed behind their ears and managed to keep their best clothes clean for the occasion. What was it about our mothers in those days that made them think the back of our 'lugholes' harboured the worst of germs? Loudspeakers on the van blared out the music as the youngsters performed traditional country dances and tied themselves in knots with the ribbons around a makeshift maypole. Each Mum looked on proudly, secure in the knowledge that it was her little 'one' who was the pick of the bunch. Just because next door's young Dorothy got poked in the eye with one of the garlanded sticks was not the fault of her child. Well, everyone knows she is accident prone. Such lovely traditions as the May Day celebrations are still with us today, but usually in the more rural areas. Morris dancers, bells a-jangling and sticks a-crashing, are a quaint sight, but one we would be the poorer without. Mummers acting out plays with storylines that are difficult to fathom about St George and physicians operating on patients, removing all manner of strange objects from their insides, are grand traditional sights. Harvest festivals and rushbearing ceremonies remind us of the days when we were in tune with mother earth and are part of our heritage that must not be lost.

Far right: Furnival Road, Balby had its bunting waving merrily in the breeze above the tables that were groaning under the weight of potted meat sandwiches, fairy cakes and bunny jellies moulded from rabbit

shaped tins. Lashings of lemonade and cups of tea were provided to wash down the feast that the mums had slaved all morning to prepare. They stood in their uniforms of flowered and floury pinafores like a regiment waiting to be inspected by Field Marshal Montgomery. On 2 June 1953 the nation celebrated in a way it had not experienced since VJ Day. We had a new queen who was being crowned and now there was the opportunity to have some fun as we started to turn the corner after shortages and belt tightening times of the immediate postwar years. These children were our future and we nurtured them with loving pride. The youngsters who were about to tuck in to the food do not look as if they suffered too much from the period of rationing that taxed their mother's culinary and budgeting skills. We will let readers decide which of the lads in the picture appears to have won the prize for being the best fed as it would not be polite for the authors to point them in the right direction!

Top right: Doncaster Royal Infirmary with its 'ever open door', as the slogan on the front float proclaimed, replaced the 1868 General Infirmary and Dispensary on Whitaker Street. The new building was opened on Thorne Road on 21 August 1930 by Lord Lonsdale. This Infirmary Sunday parade in 1934 shows gaily bedecked lorries, loaned by such local businesses as HW Jackson's, were turned into carnival floats. Marching bands, hospital staff and

voluntary groups provided an attractive sight for the hundreds of interested bystanders lining the way. A bevy of beauties sat on board one of the delightfully garlanded floats. What pretty girls Doncaster had then. Thankfully, for all red blooded males, there are still plenty around in the new millennium. Happily, some things do not change with the passing of time. Those lovelies on view in the 1930s, if still with us today, will be turned 90 by now. As they sit quietly in their armchairs they will be reflecting on that parade when they were the centre of attention, drawing admiring glances and favourable comments from the lads watching from the pavement. The cyclist alongside them was smitten. He was concentrating much harder on feasting his eyes than

watching where he was going. Who can blame him? He had won a gorgeous smile from one lass and a friendly wave from another.

Sporting life

Left: Syd Bycroft belonged to an era of Dubbin, long shorts and heavy soccer boots. His strong frame and determination carried him through the mud of a winter's pitch that modern stars would complain about as it might dirty their sponsored, white footwear. Syd's other clubs included Bradford City, Hull City and Newark, but it is with Doncaster Rovers that he played his best football. He signed in January 1936 and went on to make 442 appearances for the club. As about a quarter of these were during the war they did not count towards official records, otherwise he would have obtained a record number of games. Doncaster Rovers has its origins in the team 18 year old Albert Jenkins formed in 1879 to play against the Deaf and Dumb Institute. It joined the Midland Football Alliance in 1890 and progressed to the Midland League the following year. Rovers had two separate seasons in the Football League in the early 1900s before becoming established members in 1923. Since then the Belle Vue ground has seen many ups and downs, but the 1950s brought the most consistent period of club history when Rovers played for much of the decade in Division Two. Alick Jeffrey was one of its star players in that era. Described by Stanley Matthews as 'a boy genius', he played first team football in 1954 as a 15 year old and was representing England in a U-23 match against France two years later. Matt Busby was about to sign him as one of his famous Babes, but Alick broke a leg so badly in the international that he was never the same player again. Eventually, Busby bought another Rovers' star, goalie Harry Gregg, the hero of the Manchester United Munich disaster of 1958.

Above: Long before Bobby Charlton dreamed up his School of Excellence or soccer stars went into schools to give talks and offer some coaching, there were players who involved themselves in the community without making a fuss or seeking to profit. Here, Syd Bycroft, Doncaster Rovers' legendary centre half from either side of the last war, was helping out on the Town Fields. Power in the air was paramount for a centre half and Syd demonstrated his ability when instructing the youngsters in the art of heading. It was necessary to meet the leather ball, especially heavy in wet conditions, with the sweet spot on the forehead. Occasionally, players suffered concussion from repeated heading of something that resembled a cannonball when the ground was muddy. Centre forwards jokingly asked wingers to try to make crosses with the lace facing away from them to avoid a cut forehead. Football in the lower divisions was a tough profession and they did not come much harder than Syd Bycroft. Referees did not worry about physical contests in the way that the modern whistle blower protects the namby-pamby superstars of the 21st century. Forwards expected to be clattered by defenders. England international Tommy Lawton remembered one game against Rovers well. He described the opposing centre half as being 'big and burly' and went on to say, 'I've still got the bruises to prove it.' It was Syd at number five, of course.

Above: The men of the St John Ambulance service stood ready to leap into action in case a horse unseated a jockey. These volunteers, in their distinctive black and white uniforms, are a familiar sight at sporting events, country fairs and shows across the country. Fortunately, they were not needed on this occasion as the 1932 St Leger passed off without incident. Firdaussi, sired by Pharos out of Brownhylda, was ridden to victory by F Fox. A close second was Dastur, with jockey Beary on board. Third place went to Mrs C Rich's Silvermore with R Dick up. The Aga Khan (1877-1957), one of the most influential owners there has ever been, not only had both the first two places from his stable, but H Wragg and J Taylor rode Udeipur and Taj Kasra into fourth and fifth spots as well. Aga Khan III, also named Sultan Sir Mohammed Shah, was also a considerable political figure. He had the benefit of a mixture of western and oriental cultures in his upbringing and education that served him well in his time as a member of the Round Table Conference (1930-32) in London that advised on constitutional reform in India. Those interests took a back seat when he celebrated winning the race named after Anthony St Leger, the owner of Doncaster Home, Park Hill, and member of the group that had the idea to hold a sweepstake for three year olds.

Below: The diminutive figure, with her back to the camera in the centre of the parade ring, belonged to the woman who was 'by the grace of God, of the United Kingdom of Great Britain and Northern Ireland and of her other realms and territories, Queen, head of the Commonwealth and defender of the faith', to put it officially. To the rest of us, she is Elizabeth II. As befitted a royal figure, she was turned out in a neat suit and unostentatious hat as her position in society gave no need for flamboyance. She always appeared in public in the 1950s clutching a handbag in gloved hands. Her visit to the Racecourse continued a long line of royal interest in racing here, with particular emphasis on the St Leger, the oldest of all the English classics that saw its first winner in 1776 when Allabaculia romped home. She and her mother, the former Elizabeth Bowes-Lyon, were particularly ardent and knowledgeable followers of horse racing. The Queen's interest was inherited from her great grandfather, Edward VII. As Prince of Wales, he was a frequent visitor to Doncaster and a successful one as well. As an owner, he appeared in the winning enclosure of the St Leger on two occasions in the last years of Victoria's reign.

Shopping spree

Below: Baxtergate was widened in 1893, which is just as well because it would never have been able to cope with the increase in traffic and the swell of shoppers visiting Marks and Spencer, Alexandre and the other shops that were its main features for most of the last century. In modern times people can stroll safely along the old highway, but care had to be taken in the days when road users were not the pariahs they are now.

However, from the evidence of this photograph it would appear that the greatest danger to pedestrians came from cyclists. For the reader who is anxious about the safety of his possessions, notice how trusting we once were. There are several bikes propped up against the kerb as their riders go about their business elsewhere. There was no thought of chaining the machines to lampposts or fixing padlocks through the spokes. Repeat the scene in the 21st century and those bicycles would disappear quicker than a turkey's chances at Christmas. On the left, just beyond the dinky little carts, the Blue Bell, a Tetley's house, had been standing since at least 1819. It was rebuilt in 1880 after an explosion and underwent further major redevelopment in 1931. In its early days it occupied the whole frontage to Baxtergate.

Top: 'Meet you by Clock Corner.' How many times have those words been uttered over the last hundred years? Pals getting together, housewives meeting up with their shopping before relaxing with a cuppa in the café, a sweetheart anxiously waiting for the other to turn up or someone on a blind date looking hard for the chap with the colourful buttonhole; they all met here. Seen in the photograph that is probably from just after the second world war as Cable shoes only opened in the late 1930s, if this throng was a common sight, as indeed it was, how on earth did they find one another? The trolleybus turning the corner of the crossroads where St Sepulchre Gate, Baxtergate, High Street and Frenchgate all combine was advertising a warming brew. A mug of steaming Bovril has brought life to cold fingers and chilled stomachs on many an icy Saturday afternoon on the terraces at Belle Vue. Clock Corner, designed by JG Walker, came into being in 1895, replacing a structure that dated from 1837. It was part of the fabric of the Baxtergate widening scheme. The official opening ceremony took place on 13 February 1895 and Mayoress, Mrs F Brightmore carefully set the clock wheels in motion at precisely noon in front of Corporation representatives and a large, cheering crowd.

Above: High Street, with its jewel in the crown the Mansion House, was part of the main road through Doncaster. Here, Hallgate, Cleveland Street and Silver Street, the two women ardently discussing the main topics of the day belonged to a time when they were proud to be housewives. The politically correct brigade had not been invented and, in the 1950s, bras were only burned when they were worn out. Perhaps they were off to do some shopping at the Doncaster Clothing Company on the corner, but first they had to pass MacFisheries on the left. Tempting offers of fresh cod, caught in the North Sea before the world became concerned about quotas and stock levels, were available to encourage the women to open their purses. Friday was a popular day for such purchases, particularly among Catholic families who did without meat in their diet once a week. Our two featured ladies wore neatly permed hair in the short, tight fashion of the day. Billboard and early television adverts for a particular brand of home perm asked if we could tell which twin had the Toni. This pair spent most of the decade under the guidance of a successful Tory government that eased us from the austerity of the postwar years to the more affluent times as the spectre of those dark days of the 1940s gradually faded.

Top right: The panorama of Hallgate is shown in this photograph. Many of the people seen here would have had some connection with the railways or coal mining. These were two of the biggest industries in and around this part of South Yorkshire. The Plant Works opened in 1853 after relocating from Boston, Lincolnshire just four years after the railway reached Doncaster. The town's population increased markedly as Doncaster was transformed from a market town into an industrial centre. Although privatised and split up in the latter part of the last century, the Plant had 150 years of history building and refurbishing engines and rolling stock that were celebrated with a special open weekend in July 2003. It had given life to 2,500 locomotives and countless thousands of carriages and wagons. It was a major shock when the Canadian-owned Bombardier announced it was closing its holding in March 2004. The disappearance of the pits during the 1990s as a source of employment has added to the changes in our working

practices. A future in banking, the leisure industry, services and technology would have seemed ludicrous to these Hallgate shoppers. Surely, the country needed coal for its fires and steam locomotives to carry goods and passengers?

Right: Looking along High Street and into Frenchgate as the 1960s began, North Bridge can clearly be seen. The view is less distinct these days as the roundabout where Trafford Way and Church Way meet partly obscures our vision. The major buildings in this scene still remain to dominate the site. Clock Corner continues to be a focal spot, though Burton's famous tailoring outlet no longer trades beneath the tower. Ratner's had a period in these premises, but H Samuel, the jeweller, is there today. The handsome 1897 Midland Bank, in all its Portland stone glory beneath the green, copper clad dome surrounded by figures carved in relief, remains as a reminder to modern architects of what is meant by glorious design. The HSBC has its home here now. To the right, Baxtergate was part of the route by which trolleybuses travelled to Beckett Road and Wheatley Hills. At the start of the decade that this picture represents, our children, born in the baby boomer years of the late 1940s, were in their early teens. By the time the decade had ended their radical views on war, relationships, politics and the importance of a youthful voice in society rocked many who held entrenched, establishment views.

The private motor car was beginning to make its mark on the roads and in our driveways, as demonstrated by this 1950s' view of Hallgate where shoppers were driven in to visit the house furnishers Postlethwaite and Stacey or Meller's Dolls' Hospital. The cost of motoring came within the reach of the ordinary, working people and not the preserve of the middle classes as was previously the case. Britain threw off the constraints of those austere postwar years, employment was high and financial rewards increased as we approached Macmillan's 'never had it so good' era. As clothing coupons became a thing of the past, hemlines dropped and women took to the streets in calf length dresses and topcoats. The more intrepid even went to town bareheaded, something

their mothers would not have dared to do as they would have felt undressed. Peake's radio and piano establishment, however, showed that some fashions were slow to change. Listening to 'Dan Dare' or 'The Goon Show' was still a favourite pastime, as was a singsong when the ivories were tinkled to the tune of 'How much is that doggie in the window'. Television, though, was just around the corner. Its effect would be felt, not only by wireless enthusiasts and pianists, but by such as the proprietors of the Ritz Cinema as audiences fell. The glory days of its 70 by 30 feet café and room leading to the roof garden, plus the memories of its grand opening on 26 November 1934, when the Markham Main Colliery Band struck up manfully, were to count for little in competition with the goggle box.

© David Jamson

Left: Looking towards the corner of St George Gate, in the distance, the overhead trolley bus wires criss-crossed Baxtergate in the 1950s in front of the strong lines of the sturdy architecture that was home to the Midland Bank. Opposite Cable shoe shop, Boot's was reminding shoppers to bring their rolls of film in for processing. Initially, John Boot, who died in 1860, could never have imagined that a chain of stores would develop from a humble chemist's shop, with its simple range of medicines, as an institution on every high street. When a range of perfumes, toiletries and beauty aids was added it could have been called the 'sweet smell of success'. The desire to keep family occasions and happy holidays at the seaside alive in their memories led most families to own a humble camera. They literally took snapshots of joyous times. Today's rise in the ownership of digital cameras has taken away the excitement and anticipation of waiting for your film to be processed. It was such fun to return to Boot's counter a few days later and see the small black and white images printed out on shiny paper. Maybe

some were over exposed or a little blurry at the edges and, perhaps, mum had left her thumb in front of the lens, but they were great for reminiscing and wonderful for boring neighbours. What did it matter if Aunt Minnie's head had been cut off. Uncle Albert had been threatening to do it for years.

Above: St George's Gate, where it meets Baxtergate, had since 1760 been the site of the George and Dragon. It was rebuilt twice in the Victorian age. Despite its official name, most people referred to it as 'Beetham's', after the family that owned it for many years, and it was that name that most people recognised. Not surprisingly, 'Beetham' came to be the title written boldly on the shop front. It had been a delightful house, with tables made from beer barrels that boasted brightly polished brass hoops and tops. Interestingly, for feminists to get annoyed about, there was just a 'gentlemen's room' and no ladies! Brewers R Whitaker and Sons redeveloped the business in late 1962 when the building was revamped, but the old, familiar name retained. As a sign of the times, some catering facilities were provided for office workers to have their lunch or an early evening snack before setting off home. Sadly, the Beetham name was eventually replaced and the establishment became the Gatehouse and Mayfair Café Bar and Cellars. At least it did not suffer the indignity of being given some completely modern and ridiculous name such as the Rat and Parrot, Jumping Cricket or whatever else a brewery thinks sounds trendy, cool or wicked, or whatever the current expression is.

Below: Doncaster Health Food Shop demonstrated that, even nearly half a century ago, consideration for our dietary needs and concerns is not a modern phenomenon. However, it must be noted that healthy eating today is more of an issue as this photograph predates burger bars, microwaved meals and cola in throwaway beakers. We had our own version of fast food with fish and chips, washed down by a draught of fizzy dandelion and burdock, but at least we usually sat down at the table for our tea of cooked fresh meat and two veg, followed by a home baked pudding. It was unheard of to eat on the go or to flop in an armchair in front of the telly, plate perched precariously on one knee. This shop was on the corner of Priory Place with Printing Office Street. This latter thoroughfare was once part of the old town ditch. The derivation of its name is obvious. In 1812, the Doncaster Gazette was first printed here. Although a local paper, one of its early stories from across the continent might have featured the story of the Battle of Borodino that helped inspire Tchaikovsky's great overture, but perhaps this is too fanciful. What is sure is that, when Priory Place was established in the 1830s, it cut through the centre of the printing works. Production was moved to Market Place for a while, but eventually reappeared on Printing Office Street. This continued to be the base until the 1960s when it was moved to North Bridge.

Loaned to DLIS by Dawn White

Above: Taken c1960, this photograph of the General Market reminds us how central it has been to Doncaster's shopping life for countless generations. The hum of activity as stallholders sell their wares to crowds of keen shoppers has been an enduring feature of this spot since the Middle Ages. Some of the sights and smells may have changed, but the busy-busy nature of the market continues unabated. It first flourished on the site of the old church and expanded over its former cemetery. The market was responsible for much of Doncaster's economy in medieval times, helping it to become one of Yorkshire's most prosperous towns. People came from far and wide, such was the reputation for quality and variety. Its place as a market town of major significance continued well into the 19th century when the railway arrived. Various official charters granted Doncaster the right to hold fairs and markets. These included the 1199 Charter of King John that gave Robert de Turnham permission to have an additional day added to the already established fair on the eve of the feast of St James in July. Edward IV, in 1467, gave rights to hold a fair around the feast of the Annunciation in March and Henry VIII gave

responsibility for the administration of the market to the mayor in 1505. Subsequent charters by James I and James II expanded the role of markets and fairs even further.

Top: Hallgate in 1968 was alive with activity. Just look at all the cars parked on the left. For a traffic warden of today it would be enough to make his mouth water. The Beatles' 'Lovely Rita', the meter maid, had her pencil ready sharpened. This highway was once part of the Great North Road, so it is no surprise to see so much traffic about. For years Doncaster had been the 20th century version of a staging post. The Odeon cinema, on the left, at Nos 10-12, was part of the chain originally built up by Oscar Deutsch (1893-1941). It had begun life as the Ritz on 26 November 1934 and was the town's largest picture house with seating for 2,500 and a covered arcade with room for some 2,000 who might be queuing to get in. This was in the age of the first talkies as synchronised sound in movies was still in its infancy, having only been introduced in the late 1920s. The art deco building closed for refurbishment in April 1955 and reopened the following month as the Odeon on 25 May. Its new frontage was completely remodelled in golden flettons with its centre panel being created from concrete profile slabs. Actor Bill Owen, best known for his later TV work as Compo in 'Last of the summer wine', was one of the stars invited to the reopening. He enjoyed seeing 'The Country Girl', a movie starring Bing Crosby and Grace Kelly about the wife of an alcoholic singer who finds her own fulfilment when he makes a comeback.

Transport

Below: There it stands in all its glory, one of the shining examples of the craftsmanship that was British engineering in the last century. Flying Scotsman, with its famous number of 4472 for all to see, positively gleamed with pride as it stood in Doncaster Paint Shops prior to making the journey to Wembley Exhibition Centre. On public view in 1924, the locomotive was making its first appearance with its nameplate in place. Built the previous year by the newly formed London and North Eastern Railway (LNER), it was the first to be decked out in the soon to be famous apple green livery. This was just one of the records achieved by this magnificent giant. It was the first to pull a train on the non stop journey from London's King Cross to Edinburgh Waverley. Two drivers were used on the journey. On 1 May 1928 Albert Pidworth took the controls at King's Cross and handed over to Tom Blades on reaching Tollerton, just south of Nottingham, for the remainder of the epic run. The Flying Scotsman went on to be the first to smash through the 100 mph barrier, achieving this milestone in 1934. The locomotive was also featured in Britain's first ever talking movie, though it ran on lines rather than delivering them! These were the halcyon days of steam.

Bottom right: Cigar firmly clamped between his teeth, Lord Lonsdale shook hands with Mr RE Ford of the Doncaster Race Committee at the Racecourse in September 1927. Councillor E Wilburn stood behind them and watched the pair exchange pleasantries as race attendant Mr H Walker kept his distance in front of the horses. Lord Lonsdale's great wealth allowed him to live a life of leisure and luxury. As the first president of the National Sporting Club, which governed boxing in England from 1891 to 1929, Hugh Cecil Lowther, the fifth Earl of Lonsdale, helped establish the club as the major force in English boxing. He donated the original Lonsdale belts presented to English champions. He also had a keen interest in horseflesh and spent some years as the president of the British Show Jumping Association. As a racehorse owner he was a frequent visitor to Doncaster. Although nicknamed 'the sport of kings', it was a female monarch who donated the first royal trophy presented at the Racecourse. Queen Anne, the last of the Stuart line, gave a gold cup worth 100 guineas, a fabulous amount in the

early 18th century. The longest serving Queen of England, Victoria, never visited these races during her reign, though she was a visitor as a 16 year old when accompanying her mother, the Duchess of Kent.

Below left: The tree-lined boulevard is reminiscent of a scene from a French tourist brochure, but this was many a mile from gay Paree. The leafy thoroughfare is our own Bennetthorpe that runs from Hall Cross to the racecourse. Perhaps the special on the right was one running racegoers to and from a meeting. In 1902, not long after the first electric tram ran from Station Road, a route along Bennetthorpe was established, linking High Street with Doncaster Racecourse. It terminated at Grandstand Road, nowadays known as Leger Way. This scene, from nearly three-quarters of a century ago, was the beginning of the trolleybus era on our streets. After the tramway system had suffered neglect and a lack of maintenance during World War I, motorbuses were introduced in 1922. Some tram services were discontinued in 1925 and in the following year the Corporation decided to begin a scheme of phasing in trolleybuses on most existing tram routes. They could utilise the same overhead cabling system, but provide greater flexibility of movement and offer less disruption to other traffic. The Racecourse route was converted in 1930, though the trams were not fully eased out of the picture until 1935. Traditional motorbuses still played second fiddle to the trolleys until well after the second world war.

Bottom: A little Thomas the tank engine sits serenely centre frame, but its creator, the Reverend W Audry, will forgive us if we concentrate on the BR 60022 steam locomotive in the foreground passing Hexthorpe Bridge during realignment of the track. The sleek, streamlined shape belongs to the machine that has a unique place in railway history. As 4462 Mallard it still holds the world speed record for a steam locomotive, set on 3 July 1938. One of Sir Nigel Gresley's remarkable designs, driver Joe Duddington called to the fireman, Tommy Bray, to stoke her up. Joe opened the throttle on the slight down grade south of Grantham and the pair of Doncaster-born footplate men whizzed along until the Mallard peaked at 126 mph. Other engines have come close to matching this speed and the Americans tried to suggest that they had in the 1940s, but they would, wouldn't they. However, there was no supporting timing documentation and the Mallard's official record still stands. This LNER A4 Pacific class locomotive was in use until 1963, by which time it had covered over 1.5 million miles. It was restored to full working order in 1988 to mark the golden jubilee of its epic run. Visitors to the National Railway Museum in York can see for themselves the balance of beauty and power that made it the marvel of its age.

Left: Seen heading north for York in 1999, the 60103 Flying Scotsman had been subject to a major overhaul. In its original form as locomotive 4472, the great locomotive first came to the notice of the wider public on 1 May 1928 with its 393 mile non stop run from London to Edinburgh. It repeated the feat 40 years to the day in a special anniversary journey on the route that was established in June 1862 when the first of the weekday services left King's Cross. Flying Scotsman was designed by Sir Nigel Gresley and built at the Doncaster Works for a cost of £7,944. When it appeared in the 1929 film named after it, the locomotive had actors Moore Marriot and Ray Milland manning the controls and stoking the engine. After nearly 40 years of service it was withdrawn on 14 January 1963 and sold to Alan Pegler for £3,000, but that was not the end of the story. Like a pop music act that has run out of hit records, it went on tour in order to prolong its career. Flying Scotsman was feted in America and Australia during the 1970s and 1980s.

After several changes of ownership, Dr Tony Marchington bought it for £1,250,000 and a further £750,000 was spent in restoring it to its full glory. Subsequently based at Southall, its future was uncertain as conflicting interests from home and abroad bid for ownership.

Below: This locomotive standing in Doncaster Station was a 4-6-0 class B16/2, introduced in 1937 as a rebuild of class B16/1. The little lads on the platform bench would have known that information because they were avid train spotters. With a duffel bag full of sandwiches and a bottle of Tizer to keep them going they spent many a happy hour noting the numbers of everything that passed through. Page after page of dog-eared exercise books would be filled with dated entries of the class and model of locos, rolling stock and wagons that they had observed and duly recorded. Where are those jottings now? Perhaps they are tucked away in the loft with the Dinky cars, lead soldiers and past copies of the Beano. Maybe the lads get them down for a nostalgic moment while their wives are out shopping. Such objects help bring back the memories of the days when simple pleasures were so easy to achieve, but so precious to hold onto, if only they can. The original station was built in 1850 and had two 460 foot platforms that were used by several rail companies. As the popularity of rail travel increased it was obvious that more space was required. The station was improved and extended in late 1938 to three platforms, the longest of which measures over 1,100 feet.

© Derek Porter

Above: This photograph shows part of Baxtergate and the north side of Market Place. Nowadays, the best way to see the traditional architecture of Doncaster that did not fall foul of the developers' swathe through the town centre in the 60s and 70s is to walk with your head held high, ignoring the shop fronts at ground level. Even in the early 1950s, the top deck of a trolleybus gave a view that helped blot out the boring plate glass underneath the carefully moulded columns, cupolas, reliefs, towers and turrets that our forefathers used to heighten the beauty of the buildings they erected in our home town. The last trolleybuses ran in 1963, but their routes had been pruned from 1956 when the service to Bentley was given over to motorbuses. Children did not care whether they rode on a trolley or a motor as long as they could persuade a cheery clippie to let them have the end of a ticket roll. Evidence of payment of the fare was provided by a machine slung round the bus conductor's neck and a quick flick of a few teeth on a wheel and the turn of a handle produced a tear off piece of paper. Youngsters delighted in playing games with the numbers on their receipt. If the digits added up to five it meant that you had to kiss Danny Grimshaw, while a seven translated as 'you have a big nose'.

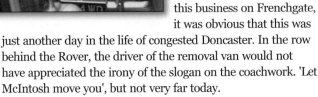

Below: The Electra Cinema, later the Regal, once occupied the lighter coloured building on the left. With its 500 seats, it was one of Doncaster's smaller picture houses, but had pride of place in being its first purpose built. Patrons waiting for the silent movie to begin might have prepared for the treat with a pint or two in the Bay Horse Inn, the next building along. By the summer of 1960 the counter attractions of television and bingo had taken their toll. Although going to the pictures was still a popular pastime, the great days had gone and the audiences with them. Eyes down and legs eleven creamed off the female over 30s, while new television shows were being launched to keep us by our firesides. There was 'Emergency Ward 10', 'Sportsview' and a serial about some Lancashire folk in a back street called Coronation Street. We liked the first two programmes, but were not sure that the other would last. When cinema audiences fell, Greenhill's drapery store took over the site. Outside this business on Frenchgate, it was obvious that this was just another day in the life of congested Doncaster. In the row behind the Rover, the driver of the removal van would not have appreciated the irony of the slogan on the coachwork. 'Let McIntosh move you', but not very far today.

Centre: The fellow in shirtsleeves was chancing his arm by dodging through the traffic on the approach to North Bridge. Risking life and limb was his only chance of getting over the road in the summer of 1960 as there were seldom any gaps in the traffic. Donny residents viewed it as part of their daily penance as they queued patiently on the way home to Bentley or Cusworth. The log jam of vehicles stretching back along Frenchgate and High Street was something to which we had become accustomed, but it was a frustrating experience for motorists and a poisonous one for pedestrians breathing in the noxious fumes. Catalytic converters and unleaded petrol were yet to come. The atmosphere had been made less toxic by the successive Clean Air Acts of the early 1950s that restricted the pollution created by industry and coal fires in our homes, but the gases coming out of car exhausts created a fug and a smell that was bad enough, even if it did not quite match the smogs we used to get ten years earlier.

Bottom: Trolleybuses first plied the journey to Balby on 26 July 1931. It was one of the busiest of all the services, carrying passengers to the south of the town centre. When these vehicles initially replaced the trams some referred to them as the 'whispering death'. Pedestrians crossing the road had been alerted to the imminent arrival of a tram by the clanking noise they made, as immortalised in song by Judy Garland in the 1944 film 'Meet me in St Louis'. The trolleybus was a different proposition. Its much quieter approach gave more than one jaywalker a nasty surprise. On its journey along Frenchgate in the 1950s, it passed the Tennant's house of the Volunteer Inn. This pub dated from at least 1760 when it was known as the Skinner's Arms, before adopting its new name early in the 19th century. Pictures of bare knuckle fighters adorned its walls and this interest in the noble art meant that its regulars often discussed famous boxers. Bruce Woodcock would have been high on the list. Born locally in 1921, he worked at the Plant and gained fame as the British, Empire and European heavyweight boxing champion in the late 1940s. Renowned for a big punch, he had 39 fights, winning 35 of which 31 were inside the distance. The Volunteer closed in 1961 and the last trolleybus ran to Balby on 8 September 1962.

The Italian job

The name Graziano may not be too familiar to many Doncaster folk but mention Carr Hill and a light bulb is immediately switched on. Graziano Trasmissioni CH Ltd, to give the company its full Sunday title, is part of the international Sauer Group of companies now with a UK base in Doncaster.

It was back in 1951 that the Graziano company was founded in Italy as a family business. Over the next thirty years the company would grow to become the major Italian 'custom' gear manufacturer with its largest customer being Fiat, this firm took more than 70 per cent of Graziano's output and with little work going to the export market. That would change over

Below: A birds eye view of the Carr Hill site, circa 1970. Below inset: Staff of International Harvesters pose for a photograph at the Carr Hill site outside what is today's Graziano Trasmissioni C H Ltd's reception. Right: Graziano Trasmissioni C H Ltd's reception, 2004.

the course of the 1980s with exports gradually increasing to half of all production. During those same years the company's research and development capability was built up; transmission components and

complete drive lines were developed (synchronisers, construction machines axles - forklift axles and transmissions). The 1980s would also see two changes of ownership with the company being acquired first by Rossi in 1986 and by Ghidella in 1989.

In 1992 Graziano Trasmissioni eventually became part of the huge Sauer Group of companies.

The Sauer Group is based in Switzerland, though with the majority of its businesses in Germany, Italy and the USA. Sauer's textile division makes it the world's largest textile machinery manufacturer, whilst the Group's total sales exceed two billion dollars annually with a workforce world-wide of more than 11,000, some 2,000 of whom are employees of Sauer's Graziano Trasmissioni Group, the group whose name now features in the story of Doncaster, Graziano having taken over the historic Carr Hill Works in 2001.

Where however, should one start the long Carr Hill story? Perhaps in 1985 when Case United Kingdom Ltd acquired the agricultural assets of Chicago-based International Harvester which at the time already had a long established relationship with Doncaster at its Wheatley Hall Road and Carr Hill manufacturing sites.

During the early part of 1965 all wheel farm tractor assembly was transferred from Doncaster Works to the newly acquired Carr Hill Works three miles away. Component parts for tractors were still made at the Doncaster Works but were sent to Carr Hill daily. This left room and freed up facilities to cope with the increasing construction equipment business at Wheatley Road. Meanwhile in those boom years some 1,500 staff continued at Carr Hill making gear shafts for agricultural machinery such as tractors, combines and trucks.

But troubles were never far off. The 1970s saw problems return for British industry: not least runaway inflation soaring to almost 30 per cent - and on its back industrial unrest as workers understandably sought to maintain the value of their wages.

This page: *Machines brought over from the U.S.A for the re-opening of the Carr Hill Site, circa 1980.*

During the eighties the company slogan was 'Build Right First Time'. The slogan was backed up by a programme designed to produce quality components and assemblies that required no costly re-working.

A scheme known as 'Pride of Performance' was developed to place responsibility for producing quality parts directly on to each operator rather than leaving quality audit to inspectors further down the line. The workforce rose to the challenge with the almost compete elimination of re-work. Any defective work was channelled immediately back the team responsible; their job was to identify and rectify the problem themselves with the support of technical staff. Special demonstrations were set up to show operators how the particular components they produced fitted into the framework of a sophisticated tractor assembly. A strong sense of co-operation and team spirit was the result.

The company's association with the Carr Hill site had began two years before farm tractor assembly was transferred there in 1965. International Harvester Great Britain announced in 1963 that it had acquired 30,000 square feet of premises at Carr Hill in Balby. A deal was struck that eventually gave the company 24 acres, so that finalised plans for the new plant provided ample room for motor truck production as well as tractor assembly.

The Carr Hill story however, went back all the way to 1888 when a railway carriage depot used for building and repairing carriages had been built on the site. The premises had subsequently been taken over by

Top left: 1998 brought a £20 million state-of-the-art machinery package with technology now used the world over. ***Top right:*** *Reishaver AZo gear grinders, the largest line of these machines in the world.* ***Far right:*** *The re-opening of the Carr Hill site by HRH the Duke of Kent, 1986.*

Briggs Motor Bodies, a firm which between 1939 and 1945 built aeroplane fuselages there for Mosquitoes and Lancaster bombers. In 1954 the Ford Motor Company had acquired Briggs Motor Bodies and subsequently used the site to build its Ford Anglia and Ford Prefect cars before selling the premises on to International Harvester.

International Harvester took possession in 1963, that momentous year in which television viewers the world over saw with horror the assassination of US president Kennedy in late November. However, that US disaster did not prevent International Harvester from arranging for all necessary equipment to be installed, so that a 1700 Loadstar, the first vehicle to be completed, left the factory gates in September 1965.

Truck production started on a regular basis in November 1965 and at first two vehicles were

completed each day. Five months later a 540 feet long production line was turning out 30 vehicles a week. By 1970 that had increased to 200 trucks a week - five trucks each and every working hour.

Tractor assembly was scheduled to begin before motor truck production. During 1964 an 880 foot elliptical assembly line was being prepared. Part of its length ran through a paint spray booth and drying ovens. Components for the tractors assembled came from an International Harvester plant in Bradford as well as from Wheatley Road, Doncaster.

In 1982 the Carr Hill site closed, with the agricultural equipment assembly work transferred back to Wheatley Hall Road. But the closure was only brief: four years later the plant was being reopened by HRH the Duke of Kent, this time to produce the high precision/ close tolerance ground gears and shafts for

the Magnum tractor at 150 horsepower and above. In 1992 the Wheatley Hall Road and Carr Hill plants merged as a one plant two site operation.

A major restructuring programme in 1994 now threatened the Carr Hill site. In 1985 International Harvester had been acquired by an old rival the Case Corporation founded in Wisconsin USA in 1842. It was now proposed that the site should either be put up for sale or be absorbed into a joint venture - or even, as a last resort, close. The work force rallied round, set up improvement schemes and raised quality standards. There were two years of uncertainty before Leopold Plattner, Case's European Managing Director, visited Doncaster and, approving of what he saw, promised that Carr Hill would remain part of Case. By 1997 Carr Hill had been allocated almost 20 per cent of Case's transmission manufacture: Case itself restructured world-wide. Wheatley Hall Road became a 'Centre of excellence' for assembly operations; transmission assembly operations were however transferred to an affiliate company in France and the foundry closed.

Meanwhile the assembly process in Doncaster was completely rebuilt at a cost of some 16 million dollars. Equipping Carr Hill with the very latest state-of-the-art

Top: *The Carr Hill site, 1997.* **Inset:** *Members of staff outside Carr Hill reception circa 1997.*

Graziano is a company passionately committed to growing the business further by delivering competitively priced, quality products on time, with a workforce totally committed to continuous improvement focused on manufacturing excellence.

Doncaster's Carr Hill plant is one of seven Graziano plants world-wide: in addition to Doncaster the company has four plants in northern Italy, one at Bari in southern Italy and one in Uttar Pradesh, India with its headquarters in Cascine Vica in Turin, or in Torino as they say it in Italian.

In the opening decade of the 21st century Graziano's Carr Hill plant's aims to be a world renowned manufacturer of gears and shafts delivering customer focused solutions. That's an aim which is certain to be achieved when Italian flair and Yorkshire know-how are combined.

equipment would cost £20 million, enabling the plant to produce the same products but to far higher specifications

In May 1997 Case held an open day to mark the official opening of the new tractor assembly facility in Doncaster. The Vice President of Case's European manufacturing operations unveiled a plaque which recognised the hard work and dedication of the company's employees who had helped create the new facility.

Change is, however, endemic and continuous in the world of international business. In 1999 Case merged with the New Holland company, which in turn led to restructuring and to the sale of the Carr Hill plant to its present owners Graziano Trasmissioni CH Ltd.

Today the two hundred or so highly skilled and motivated staff based at Carr Hill concentrate their efforts on steel-based manufacturing and engineering. The entire factory is computerised with no paperwork involved and with direct links to Turin in Italy.

Left and this page: The production of gears (right) at Graziano Trasmissioni C H Ltd using state-of-the-art machinery.

Can we have one Dad?

How many youngsters have asked if their family could have a caravan? Millions we bet. The most famous name in caravans in Doncaster is Yorkshire Caravans based in Bawtry. The firm was founded in 1930 by Percy Smith who at the time had a petrol filling station in Queens Road, Sheffield.

The business began when a caravan maker left a caravan with Percy on a sale or return basis: just two or three were sold in that first year but Percy thought caravans were better than petrol and bought two acres of land on the present site.

An ex-army hut was bought and reassembled as an office and showroom: somewhere under the more recent cladding of Percy's Bistro the old hut still exists!

In the years leading up to the second world war several agencies were obtained from differing manufacturers and what was now the Yorkshire Caravan and Trailer Company was selling up to 300 caravans a year. During the war however the business effectively closed, though service personnel, and even evacuees from London, were accommodated on the site. One of the buildings was used as an REME workshop and another large building used by an Indian regiment stationed at nearby Rossington Hall to store fodder and bedding for hundreds of their mules.

After the end of the war the popularity of caravanning increased significantly and the industry had difficulty coping; to meet demand manufacturers began supplying empty shells which were then fitted out locally with kite-marked utility furniture.

The business is now run by the founder's son Derek Smith, and his wife Jan. Their son Jon is the Service Manager whilst daughter Kate Sharpe looks after a new venture, a gift and furniture shop in addition to a thriving bistro able to seat up to 40 indoors and a similar number outside.

Yorkshire Caravans now employs 40 people and always has on display more than a hundred new and used caravans. Storage for up to 400 caravans is offered to owners who prefer not to keep their caravans at home.

And more kids than ever are asking 'Can we have one Dad?'

Yorkshire Caravans expansion plan for their Leisure Shop in 2004, includes stocking trampolines, hot tubs, jacuzzi's and mountain bikes making Yorkshire Caravans more of a complete leisure centre.

Top left: *Mr & Mrs Percy Smith, founders of Yorkshire Caravans.* ***Above:*** *An early caravan.* ***Below:*** *An early view of the site as caravanning becomes more popular.* ***Bottom:*** *The company's original site pictured in the 1930s.*

Family trees

D on't we just love our gardens? And how we appreciate garden centres such as Walkers Nurseries at Blaxton.

Lawrence Walker came to Blaxton in 1951 where he and his wife had bought a little over two acres of land on Mosham Road on which to start a nursery. The site was wet and boggy and had never been ploughed, but within two years he and his wife had raised enough crop of salad products and flowers to sell. Produce was sold to passing trade, but Lawrence would also fill the sidecar of his motorbike and take produce to Doncaster market where the Walkers had a stall.

Meanwhile the site was developed further, and the Walkers began growing roses, flowers which in the late 1950s were very much in vogue.

By the 1960s what had now become Walkers Roses had built up a stock of some 250,000 prize-winning plants.

During the 1960s nearby land which had previously been quarried was bought and a new garden created from the gravelled heaps, as well as building a shop and a house there. The centre piece of the garden was a pagoda that had once stood on top of the demolished Doncaster Co-op building in Station Road; the pagoda was rescued from the rubble by Lawrence and loaded on to his truck to be later restored to its former glory.

The nursery grew into a garden centre in the late 1960s as people began to become more adventurous with garden layouts and designs, beginning with conifers, heathers and container grown shrubs, planters and urns. The nursery won the Chelsea Flower Show's Gold Medal for its conifers in 1968. In recent years, decking, water features and garden furniture mixing with large architectural plants have come to the fore, with demand fuelled by immensely popular television programmes featuring garden improvements.

The latest garden development is a formal garden with box hedging and lily pond; many stone features have been built with old stone that was dredged from the bottom of the Don.

Three generations of the Walker family tree now work in the garden centre.

Top: Founder's, Mr & Mrs Walker. **Left:** *Walkers first Garden Centre.* **Below left:** *The greatly expanded Garden Centre pictured in 1996.* **Below:** *The pagoda rescued by Lawrence Walker which once stood on top of Doncaster Co-op.*

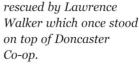

Hire and higher

DIY addicts are well aware that occasionally they need expensive equipment which it would be uneconomic to buy. The answer is to hire that costly drill or mini excavator. But it is not just the DIYer who can see the sense in hiring expensive equipment for one off jobs. The demand for such a service is even stronger in the building and engineering industries

In 1974 the firm bought premises in High Street, Bentley which not only offered clients better facilities but also enabled more staff to be employed. These new premises however were outgrown by 1979 and in that year the business moved to a former builder's yard and offices on Bentley Road behind Booth's scrap yard and the old York Road goods station.

Still a family-run company, serving the construction and engineering industry, PTE Plant Company based in Kelham Street is the oldest plant and tool hire company in Doncaster. The firm began trading in July 1972 as Power Tools & Equipment, its founders having realised the need for a local supplier of portable tools and equipment for hire or for sale. The first tool acquired was a Stihl Cutquick saw from the Stihl importer in Carlisle; the firm's founders soon found a ready demand for Stihl equipment, a demand which continues to this day.

Initially working from home and repairing tools in a garden shed the business moved to temporary shared premises until in 1973 the founders moved into shop premises in Arksey Lane, Bentley and took on their first employee.

Further power tools and items of small plant were added to the range according to customers requests. A commitment to giving customers' the service they needed as well as the equipment they needed soon led to a growing demand for the new tool hire service.

The tool hire operation was extended to include items of contractors plant adding a JCB telescopic loadall, site dumpers and generators in 1992. The business also now changed its name to PTE Plant Co.

In 1995 the Bentley Road site was to be developed for retail use making a another move necessary; as a result the present site in Kelham Street was purchased. The new premises made it possible for an even wider range of tools and site equipment to be offered from the new showroom in addition to a much improved tool repair service.

Top: A PTE Dumptruck. ***Below left:*** *A range of air conditioners supplied by Airflo.* ***Below:*** *A PTE Loadall loads into a Bradgate (sister company of PTE) screen.*

and ventilating and cooling fans. During the summer months the firm could hardly keep up with demand from all types of customers which included many well known local names, shops, offices, factories, workshops and hospitals - indeed anywhere which needed additional or emergency cooling. As a result the name of the division was changed to Airflo Enviro-rental to more clearly indicate the variety of equipment on offer.

The move to Kelham Street in 1995 provided Airflo too with the extra space it needed to improve its services and increase the range of equipment on offer. Today that range includes package air-conditioning, dust and fume extraction equipment, oil, LPG and electric heaters, dehumidifiers and specialist refrigeration reclaim equipment extending the stock of items to over 1,100. Sales on a national basis are now offered by a sister company, North & South Industries, leaving Airflo to develop the hire market using the twin slogans 'Instant solutions to relieve extreme climatic conditions' and 'Warm air, Cool air, Clean air, Fresh air, Dry air - Anywhere!'

By the middle years of the first decade of the 21st century PTE Plant had a hire fleet which includes excavators, rollers, compactor plates and dump trucks up to 12 tons, as well as a range of screening and recycling plant available from sister company Bradgate.

Top: The PTE trade counter. ***Above left:*** *Previous premises at Bentley Road.* ***Below:*** *Airflo Enviro-rental Kelham Street premises.*

But tool hire is not the only service offered from Kelham Street. Airflo Enviro-rental is a trading name of PTE. In 1981 it was decided to establish a specialist division to promote PTE's extensive range of heaters and dryers under the name of Air Dry Services. From its local depot as well as a small branch in North London the firm soon found itself with increasing demand for this specialist service.
In 1982 to increase the range of equipment it was decided to introduce portable air conditioners

Bread, meat and sandwiches

More than 30 years ago a lady from Woodlands went into a Doncaster bakers shop and, looking at the then new-fangled decimal currency, confidently predicted 'Tha knows, this new money'll never tek on'. As time has shown she was wrong, 100 pence to the pound instead of 240 is still with us. In fact some new things 'tek on' remarkably well: take that bakers shop for example.

In 1932 Mrs AM Jenkinson decided to open a small shop selling her home made cakes and toffees at 34 Hallgate in Doncaster. Business was good despite the Depression, and after a year she diversified into also making bread. Mrs Jenkinson had one employee Robert Baker who worked on the oven each night for £2 10 shillings a week.

The bread proved popular and a larger coke-fired oven was soon installed, and Mr Baker was engaged to bake during the day as well as the night.

The times were hard, millions were unemployed and ranged against Mrs Jenkinson there were dozens of competitors in the days when corner shop bakeries were the norm rather the rare exception they are today. Faced with such problems there was clearly only one thing to do: offer a better service and bake better bread and cakes than those already established bakers. Fresh, top quality food at competitive prices would be the key to building up the business - a philosophy which happily has lasted to the present day.

Before long demand outstripped the capacity of the Hallgate shop and a second shop was opened in Frenchgate

Top left: *David Jenkinson, son of the founder.*
Below: *A familiar sight to the people of Doncaster, the distinctive Cooplands shop.*

the government as a consequence of post war rationing. The price of a small loaf in 1951 was fourpence farthing (four and a quarter old pence - or around 2p today) he would recall. At the time the Mint had stopped making the farthing, which as a consequence was in short supply; young David asked a lady customer who had just fourpence in her hand 'Do you wish to owe me a farthing Madam?' to which the customer replied immediately, 'Oh no Mr Jenkinson, it's your turn to owe me a farthing!' Those were the days.

Modestly David Jenkinson would admit to having made a few mistakes in the early years and investigated developments which did not work in the long term - though many ventures and digressions, such as the company's three first-floor restaurants in Doncaster, are fondly recalled by those who used them.

Wholesaling was one blind alley which the company attempted but was unsuccessful in. It meant relinquishing control into other people's hands, and with fresh produce always likely to suffer from excessive travel and shelf storage the Cooplands maxims of quality and service were at the mercy of outside forces. The firm was not willing to sacrifice its reputation for profit.

As a result of that unhappy foray into wholesaling the company decided to stick to retail sales only through its own outlets, so ensuring that it had full control over the standards it wanted to maintain for its customers.

A new chapter had opened for Cooplands in 1951 when the firm acquired a meat allocation (one of a limited number of licences to buy and sell meat products). At the outset operations began on a small scale making hand-filled sausages. Pie fillings were soon added to the repertoire and then Cooplands expanded into cooked meats. Water immersion and Ascoli cookers were installed to produce popular favourites such as cooked ham, chicken and turkey.

in the foyer of what was the Regal cinema, very soon some ten staff were being employed.

Mrs Jenkinson was in fact laying the foundations of Cooplands (Doncaster) Ltd, a famous local company which would eventually become the dominate bakers and meat processors in the whole region, with some 57 retail outlets and over 800 staff. But why Coopland's instead of Jenkinson's? - simply that the founder chose to use her maiden name for business purposes.

Today the company Mrs Jenkinson founded has long since outgrown its original premises in Hallgate; it now operates from a 55,000 sq ft site in Milethorne Lane to where it moved in 1970. As well as a bakery the site includes meat processing, administration and a transport fleet, with some 250 staff based there.

Managing Director David Jenkinson, the founder's son, joined the business in 1948 and has led it since 1954. In those day the price of bread was still being controlled by

Top left: Batch-baking at the Cooplands Milethorn Lane bakery, 1990s. Above left: Preparing bread for delivery. Right: Cooplands meat processing department, circa 1991.

Cooked meat would eventually be sold through all the company's chain of retail shops and would come to account for almost half of annual turnover.

As more experience was gained ham curing was added to the range of skills soon followed by bacon curing - an innovation which led to the interesting discovery that in the Doncaster area 95 per cent prefer their bacon unsmoked, mysteriously the exact opposite of demand in London. Eventually even more lines would be added, such as black pudding, poloni, haslet and fresh roasted pork belly. Uncooked meat would also be sold in a few of the shops, but the focus remains on cooked products.

But man shall not live by bread (and meat) alone. He need something to wash it down with too. Around 1981 David Jenkinson queried an invoice for £30 from the Hallgate bread shop and went round to personally investigate. There he discovered that his son Michael had set up a small brewery in the back of the shop.

David was so impressed by the quality of the beer that he thought it represented another saleable commodity.

The discovery of Michael Jenkinson's mini brewery heralded the formation of Stocks (Doncaster) Brewery Ltd, a company division that would remain purposely small but which would soon acquire an enviable reputation for producing quality traditional ales. Some 60 barrels of beer were produced each week of fine, cask conditioned ale using only natural ingredients brewed under the sharp eye of head brewer Jim Butcher. Stocks Bitter, Stocks Select and Stocks Old Horizontal would go on to become prize winning beers, and be distributed through the Cameron chain of pubs in the North East.

Stocks would also eventually have three outlets of its own before Cooplands eventually decided to refocus on its central bakery and meat processing business: the Hall Cross pub in Doncaster in addition to the Turnpike in Bawtry and the magnificent Lion Hotel in Worksop a 15th century listed building with 31 bedrooms.

Top: *Cooplands Directors pictured in 1991 (left to right) William McIlroy, David Jenkinson (MD) and Peter Aldred.* ***Above:*** *Part of the company fleet, circa 1990.*

But the Cooplands name will always be synonymous with baking regardless of its other activities. Baking remains the central core of the business, and would be nearly every shopper's answer to the question 'What are Cooplands?'

Bread is the bakery's principle product, and Cooplands bakes some 32 different varieties - everything from the standard white loaf which is part of the British way of life to special loaves made to Cooplands' own recipes. One such loaf is Cooplands' High-roughage loaf, high on fibre and recommended by many doctors in the area as well as famously being promoted using the advertising pun 'All our regular customers eat Hi-Roughage'.

But bread is only part of today's output. A total of 350 lines come out of the Milethorne Lane bakery every day - savouries, cakes and sweetbreads. And not all are just

standard items turned out by the thousand: Cooplands still bake to order, and whether it is a wedding cake or a birthday surprise the bakery staff are always proud and pleased to demonstrate their skills in producing something with an individual touch.

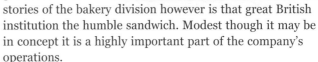

One of the greatest success stories of the bakery division however is that great British institution the humble sandwich. Modest though it may be in concept it is a highly important part of the company's operations.

Sixty thousand sandwiches a week are sold by the company, contributing millions of pounds to the business' annual turnover.

Sandwiches are freshly made to order each day in each shop and the filling for each sandwich, at least so far as the meat is concerned, brings into play the second major division of the firm - cooked meats.

Despite the appalling economic recession of the 1930s Mrs Jenkinson's small business really did 'tek on'. It surely goes to prove that old adage that you really can't keep a good man (or woman) down.

From that one small shop in Hallgate Cooplands has become a large chain, making good the company's advertising claim that 'There's a Cooplands near you'.

Top right: David Jenkinson presenting Long Service Award to Shop Manager Mrs Sheila Briggs, 2000. Above left and left: Staff prepare themselves for another busy behind the counter at Cooplands.

Learning for life

'Education, education, education' is the often repeated mantra of politicians, but education is far more just than a modern day political slogan.

Doncaster College, South Yorkshire's biggest post-16 education provider, has been meeting the educational and training needs of the area's industrial, commercial and other sectors for more than 130 years - albeit under a variety of names. The College now offers a wide range of courses, from leisure and access level provision, to postgraduate degrees and diplomas, courses which go well beyond the merely utilitarian and with a student catchment area which spans the world. The College will open the first stages of the UK's largest ever education project late in 2004.

Like much else in Doncaster the College owes its origins to the railway. In 1870 the Great Northern Railway Company GNR, alert to its own requirements for ever more skilled employees but doubtless also moved by the great Victorian tradition of philanthropy, organised evening classes in Science and Art at St James' School. The courses must have proved successful for, shortly afterwards, additional classes were arranged at St George's School and in the Mess House of the GNR works, forerunner of the famous Doncaster Plant.

In today's era of education for all it is difficult to comprehend just how great was the thirst for knowledge and self improvement amongst the working classes in late Victorian times. Many of those who attended evening classes were the first generation of their families who had been able to read and write. Anyone who looks through the marriage registers of say the 1850s will quickly see that many of those who had just taken their marriage vows would sign the register only with an X.

But that situation was set to change with a number of Education Acts which provided for at last a minimum of education for everyone. Children may still have left school at 12 or even younger to work in the mining industry and factories, but by then they had at least mastered the minimum skills, reading, writing and arithmetic, necessary to permit them to aspire to greater things. Working folk who had lived in the shadow of ignorance and who had to rely on their betters to read and write letters for them, and who relied on others to tell them what was going on in the world, could now read it for themselves in newspapers whose sales were surging in the face of the new mass market for printed material.

Top: *Doncaster Education Department.*
Right: *Doncaster College of Technology pictured in the 1970s.*

Though the primary education offered to everyone may have been rudimentary it provided the minimum tools necessary to better oneself and created a demand for even more precious knowledge. In an age when further education was a rare commodity it was sought after and valued to a degree which is almost inconceivable today. And not just for its own sake: knowledge is power.

Trades Unions were well aware of the value of education and that its acquisition would allow working men to deal as equals with employers and the upper classes who managed and owned businesses and who governed the country. For this reason if no other, socialists of all hues supported and encouraged further education quite as much as those business leaders who, for reasons of their own, wanted a well educated workforce.

Just seven years after the GNR's early initiative a dedicated Art School was built in Doncaster above the Free Library, and all existing evening classes were transferred there or to premises adjacent to the Old Grammar School buildings: Mr Hartley was the Master in Charge.

In 1902 Mr George Grace was appointed first Principal of Doncaster Technical College. At this time classes were held in the Old Vicarage near the College and in other buildings in the town. Mr James Eagles succeeded Mr Grace in 1907.

As Doncaster's industries flourished in the years before the Great War the number and variety of classes increased greatly. More space was needed and a new College building was started at Church View in 1913. The outbreak of the first world war in 1914 however delayed completion of the new building and it was not occupied until 1915.

By 1918 it was evident that education for work must start at an earlier age. A new Junior Technical School was established, headed by Mr Herbert Wilson, and continued as part of the College until 1944. As well as achieving excellent results in its own right the Junior Technical School proved a ready source of suitable students for the College. During this period the College also hosted part-time day and evening Technology classes whilst the School of Art continued to flourish in a separate building.

When Doncaster became a County Borough in 1927 the new borough council took over the management of the College from the West Riding County Council. The academic year 1929-30 saw 1,173 students registered in some 187 classes. The following year Mr George Lawn succeeded Mr Eagles on the latter's retirement.

Student numbers continued to grow and in 1934 the premises were considerably extended yet again, at a cost of £46,000 for buildings and £20,000 for equipment. In recognition of the College's importance to local industry and employment the Miners' Welfare Fund contributed a generous £14,700 towards the cost.

Meanwhile classes were also being held at Sunny Bar, Elmfield House, the Grammar School and the Technical High School for Girls. Further expansion plans, drawn up in 1937-39, were once more thwarted by war and yet more 'temporary ' accommodation was requisitioned, including an auction room, a bakery, a

day nursery, Co-operative Society rooms, a church hall and pre-fabricated huts.

Post-war, returning service people clamoured for qualifications to prepare them for the peacetime world. And what a peacetime! The fathers of returning servicemen, the older generation which had fought in the trenches of Flanders and who had returned home in 1918, had been promised a land fit for heroes. All their hopes had been cruelly dashed: in the early 1920s many had enrolled for educational course to fit them for jobs in that heroic new world. What they got instead however was mass unemployment and poverty.

Happily the post wars years of the 1940s and 1950s would be a far different experience from the 1920s and 1930s. The Labour Government elected in 1945 really was going to create a world fit for heroes. The most revolutionary government ever elected in modern times set out to not only create institutions such as the

Elsewhere, Doncaster College of Education, dedicated to teacher training, was founded in 1949 by the County Borough of Doncaster Education Committee; it moved in the following year to High Melton.

There can have been few if any decades more propitious than the 1950s though perhaps it only seems so in hindsight. Oldsters who had seen brief post-war prosperity collapse so quickly in the 1920s just shook their heads pessimistically - if things were good now it was only a sign that they would soon be getting worse. But for younger folk, those too young for the war, the world was now beginning to come right and could only get better. The start of the decade saw the coronation of the beautiful young Queen Elizabeth II and the dawn of a new Elizabethan age. Yes there were problems, the Suez Crisis and the Korean War but they were far away events; what mattered in Britain was that everything was getting better and better. Even the music was improving and by the mid 1950s Rock and Roll could be heard for the first time at Doncaster College dances. No doubt Prime Minster Harold Macmillan didn't have Rock and Roll in mind when he pointed out in a famous speech that we'd never had it so good - but he was right not just about the economy and music but about education too.

Top left: *Doncaster College of Education, 1990s.*
Below: *Students take a break in the college canteen.*

NHS and the Welfare State but also to nationalise much of British Industry - not least coal and the railways both central to Doncaster's prosperity.

And, unlike in the 1920s, when a brief upsurge in the economy had created false hope, this time prosperity would last for two decades or more. That ever increasing prosperity would fuel even greater demands for further education.

In 1947-48, as Mr Hugh Richmond succeeded Dr Lawton, some 4,850 students enrolled in 985 classes but, inevitably, a routine inspection found the College once more hampered by lack of space. Church View was extended yet again and it was suggested that the Secondary Technical School move out - even so, new premises on a larger site were essential. The same inspector's report suggested that a proper College Library be established, and also commented on the College's excellent social activities, especially those associated with the Dramatic Art section.

By 1958-59 some 6,228 students had enrolled at Doncaster Technical College under its principal, W Lomax. There were by now departments of Mechanical Engineering, Mining, Electrical Engineering, Science, Commerce, Building, Household Science, Dramatic Art and Physical Education in premises at St George's Gate, Waterdale, East Laith Gate, South Parade, Netherhall Road, the BR Plant canteen and Wheatley Hall Mines Rescue Station, amongst other locations.

Phases I-IV of the long-awaited new Waterdale premises, adjacent to the then - Waterdale bus station, were erected between 1958 and 1963 whilst the new Waterdale frontage was added in 1965.

The 1960s and 1970s would witness an interesting revolution in the attitude to education and in the appearance of students. Full employment and the arrival of a generation unfamiliar with service in the armed forces - and an expectation of an education at the expense of the state - would produce a startlingly different type of individual. Gone were short back and sides and neat clothing; in came long hair and jeans. Out would go demure dresses for girls and in would sweep mini-skirts

Above, both pictures: *Students perfecting their computer skills.* ***Below:*** *An artists impression of state-of-the-art facilities for Doncaster Education City.*

and make-up. Though many, indeed most, students remained hard-working and were diligent at their studies, the hunger for education so evident in previous generations had visibly been assuaged by familiarity. Not until the harsher, more competitive times a generation later would personal commitment to education become once again more intense.

The College of Technology, College of Art and two other colleges were integrated in 1976 to form the Doncaster Metropolitan Institute of Higher Education (DMIHE) a body which offered both further and higher education courses. Maintained by Doncaster Local Education Authority it became the major provider of 16-plus education in the Borough and received its own governing body in 1978.

Don Valley Institute of Higher Education (DVI) was established in 1980, primarily as an Adult Education institute on the pattern of the former West Riding institutes. It was reorganised in 1988 and merged with DMIHE in 1990 to form Doncaster College.

An independent institution, the newly incorporated College was operated by the Doncaster College of Further Education Corporation under Principal Terry Ashurst, who had been appointed the previous year to implement the change. By now the College had 12,000 students, on six widely scattered sites. Those six sites quickly rationalised to five: Waterdale, Church View, High Melton, Mexborough and Bessacarr. That was a major improvement on the no fewer than 12 sites which had been in use as recently as 1985 - though the operations of the former DVI would continue to involve outreach operations within many other organisations' premises throughout the Borough.

Progress would never stop: in 1992 the Dearne Valley Business School was established at High Melton with £820,000 of City Challenge money.

Terry Ashurst retired in 2001 after a period of major expansion and development, being succeeded by Dr George Holmes.

Dr Holmes would be tasked with implementing the next major project, the establishment of 'Doncaster Education City' - DEC. This will involve the rationalisation of the Waterdale and High Melton operations, on an exciting new riverside site adjacent to but across the River Don from Church View and incorporating a Doncaster University College.

The aim of Doncaster Education City is to transform the Borough of Doncaster from an area of limited job opportunities and increasing social deprivation into a thriving community with good standards of living and a workforce capable of undertaking the high quality professional jobs that will be generated by complementary projects such as Finningley Airport. The resulting improved infrastructure of education and training provision will also ease the path for other industries to move into the area and in this way link education and training to Doncaster's regeneration agenda.

Education is the key to both personal advancement and the advancement of our whole community. Today, as always, Doncaster College is doing its best to ensure that both Doncaster and its inhabitants have that key.

Top: *An artists impression of Doncaster Education City.*
Left: *Dr George Holmes.*

Days at the races

There are few events to compare with the excitement and spectacle of a day at the races. And at Doncaster Races there's an atmosphere second to none. With 29 days of first class racing each year to choose from, not least the St Leger Festival in September, everyone is guaranteed an unforgettable experience.

Doncaster is one of the oldest established centres for horse racing in Britain, with records of regular race meetings going back to the 16th century. In 1600 the corporation tried to put an end to the races because of the number of ruffians they attracted, but by 1614 it acknowledged failure and instead marked out a racecourse.

At the start of the 18th century the corporation even paid for an annual trophy - the Corporation Plate.

The earliest really important race however was the Doncaster Gold Cup, first run over Cantley Common in 1766, ten years before a move to the racecourse's present location.

During the earliest years of the St Leger horses tended to be local - though some horses would be walked for up to six weeks from as far away as Newmarket to take part. The race is named after Lieutenant Colonel Anthony St Leger (then pronounced 'sellinger') an Irish soldier who between 1763 and 1780 lived at Park Hill, Firbeck near Doncaster.

Meanwhile thieves, pickpockets, card sharps and ruffians of all kinds continued to infest the racecourse: in 1829 they rioted and had to be dispersed by the military. In later years

*Top: An early running of the St Leger, the world's oldest Classic horse race. **Above:** William Scott, rider of nine St Leger winners between 1821 and 1846. **Left:** The (listed building) Clock Tower Stand.*

policemen from all parts of the country would be drafted in to keep good order.

The huge crowds which were to become a feature of the St Leger began to appear after the rail link to Doncaster was completed in 1849: in 1876, the St Leger's centenary, no fewer than 233 special excursion trains brought racegoers to the town.

Many of the social elite, including the Prince of Wales, the future Edward VII, would arrive in Yorkshire from all over the country.

Visitors would also include thousands of Yorkshire miners and their families who made the St Leger their special holiday in the late 19th and early 20th centuries. Pits would shut down and for a little while cloth caps replaced the top hats of the gentry

During the first world war the racecourse was used for military purposes and substitute races were run at Newmarket from 1915 to 1918. More happily in the second world war racing was only cancelled in 1939.

Doncaster has the distinction of both starting and ending the Flat season on turf. After 20 days of Flat racing there follows 9 days of National Hunt racing in the winter months: the Great Yorkshire Chase is the feature event which has seen many Grand National horses in the line up over the years.

Known to many racecourse goers as 'Sunny Donny' Doncaster is the only racecourse in South Yorkshire and one of the most active in the country. Doncaster is justifiably proud of being the home of the St Leger the world's oldest Classic race dating back to 1776 and which is traditionally run on the final day of the September Festival.

The winner of the 1886 St Leger, and arguably the best horse of the whole 19th century, was the famous Ormonde, eventually sold to the USA Stud for £30,000 - then an extraordinary sum. Not until Nijinsky won the St Leger in 1970 would racegoers see Ormonde's like again.

Other well-established races are the Park Hill which began in 1971 a race for fillies-only run over the Leger distance, and the five furlong Portland Handicap first staged in 1855. A newer important race for two-year olds has

assumed various names, most recently the Racing Post Trophy.

Doncaster has also hosted events whose traditional homes have closed down, such as Lincoln in 1965 and Manchester the previous year. More history was created at Doncaster in 1992 when it staged the first ever Sunday meeting on a British race course: a crowd of over 23,000 turned up despite there being no betting.

Today, after more than four hundred years of racing, Doncaster racecourse, the home of the St Leger, can surely claim a place as a national treasure.

Top: The great Lester Piggott and wonder horse Nijinsky win the 1970 St Leger. **Below:** *Pat Eddery rides Silver Patriarch to victory in the 1997 St Leger, his fourth St Leger winner and his 4,000th career victory.* **Bottom:** *Huge crowds enjoying the excitement and atmosphere at the St Leger Festival.*

Lighting up times

Vans bearing the slogan 'Smith Bros Electrical Distributors' are a familiar sight around the town of Doncaster. But where do they come from and where are they going? Where they are coming from is an easy enough question to answer, they are all from the Smith Bros Main Distribution Centre, Friars Gate, Doncaster. As to where they are going to - well these days that could be anywhere in Britain.

The firm of Smith Bros (Caer Conan) Wholesale Limited to give the company its full Sunday-best title is one of the United Kingdom's largest stockists and distributors of discharge lamps, control gear and a compete range of electrical installation materials made by the industry's leading manufacturers. The company specialises in supplying local authorities, street lighting contractors, health authorities, electrical contractors and utility suppliers with street lighting equipment and related electrical products. But many of these products did not exist when the company started.

In fact the business can trace its origins back to before Wellington's victory over Napoleon at the battle of Waterloo, all the way back to January 1814 when one

William Radford Bayliffe opened an ironmongery shop at 14 High Street, Rotherham.

Bayliffe, who was the son of the vicar of Rotherham, ran the firm until 1840 when the original Smith brothers took over - and renamed the business after themselves.

The ironmongery business attracted many customers, not least the Earl of Effingham who became so impressed with a wire riddle he bought from the High Street shop in Rotherham that he became widely known by the nick-name of 'Wire Riddle Richard'.

The firm became a limited company in 1890 - GS Smith becoming its Managing Director - and expanded, acquiring warehouse premises in The Crofts.

Left: Smith Bros Ironmongers, 1908.
Above: Early company stamps.
Below: E J Morris, founder of post war Smith Bros.

In 1902 a branch was opened at 108 Broad Street, Parkgate. Three years later Smith Bros Ltd was advertising itself as 'Wholesale Ironmongers, Iron and Steel Merchants, Mill Foundry and Colliery Furnishers'.

By the time of the business' centenary in 1914 both of the original Smith Brothers had passed away, but it was still business as usual despite the outbreak of the Great War with Germany and her allies. In its adverts the company boasted of being able to obtain 'almost anything in the hardware trade... from a mousetrap to a steam engine'. That unlimited promise had already seen the firm venturing into many different areas, far beyond the original ironmongery service - such as becoming the first firm to offer the bicycle to the Rotherham public. In fact so comprehensive was the stock carried that it even included several makes of motor car accessories as well as hundreds of different sized screws. Smiths even installed electric lighting in numerous churches, including Rotherham Congregational Church.

It was from these origins that today's Smith Bros (Caer Conan) Wholesale Ltd was born when a Doncaster branch of Smith Bros was opened in Silver Street in 1925.

The 'Caer Conan' part of the company name was borrowed from another company, Caer Conan Ltd, owned by a Director of Smith Bros Rotherham, Thomas Cocker. The name comes from the Ancient British name that was eventually changed to the modern 'Conisborough'. The addition of Caer Conan to the already-established Smith Bros name had the advantage of marking it out from numerous other Doncaster firms with a similar name. Of the new company's 1,000 shares 999 were owned by Caer Conan Ltd and just one by Thomas Cocker personally. The new company began in the same manner as its parent company, selling a variety of different products such as gas, electric and domestic appliances as well as radios. Traditional iron and steel products were also sold from the new Doncaster premises, such as pots, pans and cutlery.

Smith Bros (Caer Conan) Wholesale became a separate limited company in 1932: The Smith Bros' Rotherham boss, Thomas Cocker, along with Harold Copley, were appointed as its first directors. This then was the year that the real story of Smith Bros (Caer Conan) Wholesale Ltd began. A new employee, 20-year-old Ezra John Morris, who was later to become affectionately known as 'EJ' started a summer job with the firm that same year; he went on to become

Managing Director and ultimately its owner and Chairman, guiding the firm to eventually become the multi-million pound countrywide concern it is today.

For most businesses the 1930s were period of stagnation or even failure. The stock market crash of 1929 precipitated a world-wide recession which would last decades. Happily despite the general trade recession, unlike many of its business competitors, Smith Bros rode the storm and even grew.

Around 1936 the company moved into Market Road and to the distinctive curve fronted shops under the Sunny Bar clock. Here the firm was able to expand further; employees were often seen around the town making deliveries with handcarts and bicycles. Later in that same year Harold Copley resigned and Thomas Cocker's wife Kate took his place as a Director.

During the war years trade was very difficult, and like many other firms Smith Bros was even forced to resort to selling 'under the counter' stock, such as batteries, just to keep the business going. During those years further changes were also made to the management with Mrs Rose May

Nicolson becoming a Director in 1940 followed by 'EJ' Morris four years later. The founder of the Doncaster company, Thomas Cocker, had died in 1943 leaving just the two new Directors in charge when his grieving widow resigned from the Board in 1944. Both EJ and Mrs Nicolson received 400 shares each of the company's 1,000 shares.

After the war Smith Bros began to thrive once more, especially with the increasingly widespread use of electricity which the firm was quick to supply. Smith Bros employees were encouraged to visit local companies such as International Harvesters (which later became JI Case) to drum up business. International Harvesters, which was already well known in the Doncaster area, was however then little more than a farmhouse: an order for six light bulbs from the firm was considered a big deal at the time.

Smith Bros would supply wholesale electrical items to just about every major Doncaster firm such as

Top: *Smith Bros Main Distribution Centre from St George Bridge.* ***Above:*** *A view inside the warehouse.*

Peglers, and were themselves customers of Brook Crompton. The firm prided itself on its competitive prices and high quality of service.

Increasing sales were undoubtedly helped by better transport. The post war years saw the end of staff using bicycles. EJ Morris' own Rover was bought by the company in 1945 for use as a company car whilst a new Bedford van was bought in 1952 for £513. The share capacity of the company was increased from 1,000 to 19,000 £1 shares in 1958 which were divided between EJ and Mrs Nicolson

By the early 1960s the Market Road premises which had been occupied since 1936 had become too small for the flourishing company, forcing it to relocate to the former Waterways Depot on Greyfriars Road where it remains to this day. The depot had once been the centre of a thriving canal transport system that supplied coal from the nearby collieries to power stations throughout the country. The creation of the motorways during this period had resulted in coal transport switching from barges to lorries and so creating an ideal town centre location for Smith Bros to conduct its business. The distinctive 'Tom Pudding' barges are still occasionally seen from the office windows, although leisure and domestic ones are now more common following the redevelopment of the dock area.

Meanwhile just after the move to Greyfriars Road the company became more of a family concern when both EJ's wife Mary, and his brother Samuel Mandy Morris, were appointed as Directors at the same time as another new Director, Noel E Smith.

Above: Smith Bros fleet outside the Main Distribution Centre, Friars Gate. Below: A group of Staff members at the Main Distribution Centre.

This was time of national growth and improvement which the company was quick to capitalise on. With the appointment of the current Managing Director, Peter Jervis, as Technical Manager in 1964 the company began moving away from domestic appliances and began specialising more in street lighting, winning contracts and supplying Public Authorities throughout the length and breadth of Britain.

In 1965 it was decided to increase the share capital of the company from £20,000 to £30,000 by the creation of 10,000 new shares of £1 each. Those ten thousand shares were allocated equally between EJ Morris and Mrs Rose M Nicolson giving them each a holding of 15,000 shares. Later that year 14,900 of Rose M Nicolson shares were sold to EJ Morris and the remaining 100 to Constance Mary Morris who was then made a Director of the company.

During the 1970s the company continued it's expansion, securing contracts with the Yorkshire Electricity Board and Electrical Contractors. Towards the end of that decade space was once again becoming a problem as the firm expanded into the health sector supplying electrical and lighting goods to hospitals and clinics. When a former newspaper printing works became available on the opposite bank of the canal offering much needed space for expansion Smith Bros seized the opportunity to create extra storage space.

The Bulk Storage Unit as it became known would be extended three times since it was acquired, becoming the main storage and distribution centre for the company. This expansion into new premises (which would become linked by telephone, and later by computer terminals) allowed extra office space in the Canal Depot premises and provided a more pleasant working environment for employees.

By the Diamond Jubilee of the company in 1985 the company could look back on 60 years of continuous evolution. At the beginning there had been just four or five staff selling mainly household products and making deliveries by bicycle : by the time of that Diamond Jubilee the business had become a major electrical wholesale supplier with some 80 staff and 15 delivery vans. There had also been a new addition to the board of directors the previous year with the appointment of Richard Bielenica who had joined the firm in 1969. Coincidentally that Diamond anniversary was also shared with a product that had been highly influential in the history of the company - the Philips Sox Lamp, a low pressure sodium lamp used for illuminating highways all over the world.

EJ Morris died in August 1996 at the age of 84. He had worked right up to his death, still showing the same

Top: *Smith Bros Canal Depot.*

determination and hard work that had moulded the company from being a small gas, electric and radio wholesalers selling domestic appliances into a nation wide provider of lighting, cable and fittings. Most of the changes in the company's history had been influenced by this man, and despite his sometimes over-ambitious plans and economic upswings and downturns he had never made a single member of staff redundant. In fact the loyalty not only to EJ personally but also to the company as a whole would lead to a large number of its employees qualifying for long service awards, employees such as Mark Jervis who joined the Company in 1975 as a Trainee Manager and became a Director in 1991 and Nancy Sheach who joined the Company in 1968 as an Accounts Clerk, became Office Manager and was appointed to the Board of Directors in 2003.

Since EJ Morris' wife and brother had died before him his death posed a major problem for the company. Not only had the firm lost an influential leader, but equally problematic the majority share which EJ had held in the business now passed to distant relatives who had little interest in Smith Bros. To save the company from a take-over or any other outside interference it was agreed that there would be a management buy-out, allowing the firm to pass into the hands of those who were already responsible for its day to day running.

Today's four shareholders Peter Jervis, Richard Bielenica, Mark Jervis and Nancy Sheach remain committed to providing the same high standards and commitment to the firm's employees and customers that Smith Bros (Caer Conan) Wholesale Ltd has always provided.

The year 2005 will mark the company's 80th anniversary of service to its customers in Doncaster and further afield. An article in The Advertiser dated 10th January 1914 described the company of Smith Bros Rotherham as already running for a hundred years, and added that 'it looks like going on forever'. The company may have changed its stock, location and its management many times over but it is that ability to change with the times and to meet the varying requirements of its customers which has allowed Smith Bros (Caer Conan) Wholesale Ltd to remain an important business in Doncaster's past. The Directors, Management and Staff now look forward to the future and the challenges of the 21st Century.

Below: *Left to right, Nancy Sheach, Neil Dawson, Kevin Banks, Mark Jervis, Maurice Ockleford, Richard Bielenica, Helen Williamson, sitting Peter Jervis. This small group represents 266 years of service with Smith Bros (Caer Conan) Wholesale Ltd.*

Individual by design

The surname Lewis is one of the most popular names in Britain. The name arrived in England as a Christian name along with the Normans in 1066 and was originally derived from the Old Frankish name Hludwig meaning 'loud battle'. In Wales the name was used as a shortened form of Llewelyn, itself derived from the Welsh word Llyw meaning 'leader'. The Welsh use of hereditary surnames only began in the 16th century when the normal practice became to take the father's name as a surname such as in Madog ap Llwelyn - Madoc son of Lewis. Today Doncaster's leading home builder Lewis Homes (Yorkshire) Ltd features the black lion rampant, the central motif on the Lewis coat of arms, as a 'signature' on many of its new homes, a feature either set into the external brickwork or discreetly embellishing the turned newels on feature staircases.

Older readers who may just recall the days when it was still possible to buy a house in Doncaster for £600, were astonished in 2003 when new luxury homes appeared in Doncaster, the like of which had never been seen before. Built

Above: Founder David Lewis pictured with his dog Penny in the 1970s. Right: David Lewis is presented with a pair of safety boots as top Wimpey Apprentice of the year, 1968. Below: An example of Lewis luxury homes.

on Bawtry Road, one of Doncaster's prime locations, by Lewis Homes the new homes sold for an astonishing £650,000 - a record for Doncaster.

Lewis Homes (Yorkshire) Ltd is a local company owned by David Lewis. David is the son of a miner and was born in South Wales in 1948, though he moved to Doncaster at the age of five.

After leaving school at the age of 15 David moved back to Wales to work as an apprentice brick-layer in his family's small building company.

David was 18 at the time of the Aberfan disaster when thousands of tons of old colliery waste fatally slipped down a mountainside to engulf the local junior school. David was one of those called in to help dig out the school which had been all but buried. After two days of digging in water David was left

with pneumonia and pleurisy.

Told that because of his ill health that he might never lay bricks again David began to attend additional college courses in management, and was transferred as a trainee to G Wimpey Ltd where he won numerous awards and prizes for his efforts including a Junior Chamber Overseas Travel Award in 1969.

In 1970, at the age of 22, David married his wife Jennifer and moved to Doncaster to begin work at HOC in Scunthorpe before moving first to Firths and then subsequently to Wellmar. In 1979 David got a telephone call from Peter Ravenhill who asked him to join his building firm, Ravenfield Construction. David formed a close bond with Peter Ravenhill who tragically died from cancer in the 1980s. On Peter Ravenhill's death David Lewis was able to take over the business and he would continue to trade under that name for many years.

Ravenfield Construction had been founded in 1978 and originally operated from Netherall Road in Doncaster before moving into the next street, to 54 Copley Road in the mid 1980s. The company bought the premises next door, number 56, in the mid 1990s and knocked through to create a larger office. In the summer of 2002 however the company moved to prestigious new offices at Saddlers House, South Parade Bawtry which remain the Lewis headquarters today.

Doncaster residents who have been watching the progress of the company will, over the years have seen new homes go up in Bonby, Auckley - where at Dursley Court a local schoolgirl

won a competition to name the street, which she named after her late father , Chadwick Gardens, Arksey, where the firm built its first vicarage, Ealand, Misterton, Wheatley, Bircotes and Ranskill.

Meanwhile an eight home apartment block at Blaxton, completed in 2002, was given the name Talliswen House. The Lewis family have always had an interest in pedigree dogs. In the 1940s and 1950s David Lewis' grandfather and his brother successfully exhibited Welsh and Scottish terriers. David continued the family tradition and bred Welsh Springer Spaniels. He organised the first show for Welsh Springers in the North of England in the 1970s. David exhibited his dogs under the name of Talliswen, a name which combined the names of two streets on the Rhondda Valley in South Wales where he had been born.

Being a child in the 1950s before the days of a Playstation, David like many of his contemporaries spent hours logging the names and numbers of steam locomotives. His spotter book survived and is used today to name the developments and house names.

Top left: David Lewis opens the Vicarage that Lewis Homes built on their Chadwick Gardens development in Arksey. Centre: The Lewis Coat-of-Arms. Many of the Lewis homes carry a hand crafted Coat-of-Arms carved in the brickwork or discreetly embellished on the turned newels of the feature staircase. Top right, left and below: More examples of Lewis homes.

Most of Lewis' developments are based on the ideal of small, exclusive developments, usually no more than seven properties. The company has a unique approach to house building in that it is very flexible in the design of its houses, allowing customers to have a large input into the design of their homes - it is very much a bespoke service

Today the business is made up of three main companies: Lewis Construction, Lewis Homes and Lewis Building Services.

Lewis Homes (Yorkshire) Limited, founded in 1987 as L & S Homes, before changing its name in 1995, is the residential house building arm of the company.

Lewis Construction (Yorkshire) Ltd changed its name from Ravenfield Construction in 1995 and is the contracting arm of the group; it carries out refurbishments of listed buildings as well as undertaking industrial and commercial projects for major clients. Finally Lewis Building Services (Yorkshire) Ltd, also formed in 1995 is the newest company in the group, it provides health & safety advice and training to other companies in the group as well as to other companies in the industry, and indeed in other industries too.

By the late 1990s the business was building some 40 to 50 properties a year; prices by then were starting from as little as £85,000 for a four-bedroomed detached house. The company was enjoying a £4 million annual turnover thanks to specialising in the luxury homes market. Over the years the company had carved out a major niche for itself in the marketplace based not simply on building luxury

homes but also by building homes for the kind of individuals who like to express themselves in the way they want their houses to look, feel and function.

Based on small individual developments - about six to an acre - customers were and continue to be, positively encouraged to make their feelings known about all the details that make life more comfortable. Though the company never set out to be different by concentrating on giving customers choices in a highly competitive market that 'unique selling point' of offering choice upon choice was a way forward which simply evolved in response to market forces - and to David Lewis' deep conviction that a personal service was what discerning home buyers really wanted as much as quality and value for money.

Dedicated staff are trained to discuss with clients the practicalities and feasibility of their ideas, whether they want to change the shape of a room, have a pit in the garage, a loft conversion or underfloor heating. All they have to do is decide what they want, discuss it with the company's staff and then sit back and watch their dream home rise from its foundations.

This page: *Examples of previous Lewis Homes' interiors.*

The company of course also believes in offering value for money and quality: it invites prospective buyers to inspect its work and compare it with anything that can be provided by well-known national competitors.

Today David Lewis' reward for all his hard work is having time to travel and watch sport. Being Welsh rugby is a great passion: a former player himself he is a regular visitor to Cardiff's Millennium Stadium. Ice hockey too is a favourite pastime and David had held a season ticket for more than decade: Lewis Homes enjoy a suite at the Sheffield Arena where colleagues, customers, and business accuaintances enjoy the sport.

David Lewis' son Justin now lives in New York with his wife Lynnette and son Dylan. Daughter Sian, however after completing her university education has joined the business as director of the newly formed land buying company.

While he has become a grandparent, David's ambition has not diminished; the company has grand plans for the future.

Current plans for a luxurious apartment block of 17 individual properties in Doncaster are on the drawing board. The scheme will include a concierge service, a fully equiped gymnasium, and a dedicated laundry room.

The Willbrook house type that was successfully launched on Bawtry Road in 2003 has been modified and upgraded to be developed at a super location in nearby Ranskill in 2004.

David is convinced that the advanced technology that is available should be built into new homes. He believes that new homes should learn from the advances made in the motor industry and that property should evolve and advance in the same way the motor car has. You would not dream of buying a new car without central locking and electric windows, so why put up with old technology in new homes.

Top (both pictures) and left: Artist impressions of Lewis Homes' Bawtry Road luxury homes.
Below left: The future-proposed new Doncaster luxury apartments. Below right: The future generation, David Lewis' son Justin, daughter-in-law Lynnette and grandson Dylan.

Howzat! a century of estate agency

For any firm to be celebrating a hundred years in business is something to be proud of. And the firm of estate agents C Barnsdale & Son are understandably proud of their long service to the people of Doncaster.

It was at the turn of the 20th century that Charles Barnsdale first came to Doncaster with his parents from Nottingham, where he had worked for Jesse Boot, the founder of Boots the Chemists. Charles set up offices in Copley Road in 1905, managing the property affairs of the Flowitt family who had been major builders of many late 19th century Doncaster houses.

In the late 1920s Charles' son Frederick joined him and the business moved to larger premises in Netherhall Road; shortly afterwards Frederick's sister, Norah, also joined the firm to work in the accounts department.

By the 1960s Frederick's son Malcolm had joined the firm permanently; he had already helped his father many times during school holidays. Malcolm, born in 1941, had made no decision about going into the family business when he went off to study at Worksop College, but it must have been in the blood. Malcolm's first job was rent collecting following the death of the rent collector. The rent collector had died at Christmas 1960 and fortuitously Malcolm was due to join his father and start work on New Year's Day 1961.

For three days a week Malcolm collected rents from around a thousand properties in an area around Doncaster that included Balby, Hexthorpe, Bentley, and Hyde Park. At this time a larger number of people still rented their homes as only the well to do could afford to buy their own houses. Three quarters of the firm's business in those days concerned property management.

There were few other staff when Malcom joined the firm: his father Frederick carried out all the valuations and surveys himself. The firm's founder Charles Barnsdale died in April 1961, proud and happy to know that the third generation had joined the family business.

The firm continued to grow and as business flourished through the 1960s and extra staff were engaged. House sales increased, as did the property management department which handled many hundreds of properties throughout the area.

Increasing prosperity saw many Doncaster folk who would never previously have bought their own home now entering the property market for the first time. Naturally they bought and sold their homes through the well established estate agency of Barnsdale & Son. It's hard to believe now, but at the start of the 1960s it was still possible to buy a small house for under

Top left: *Founder, Charles Barnsdale.*
Right: *The firms Netherhall Road office, 1906.*

Continued growth has resulted in Paul Wildsmith being appointed a Partner dealing with residential management.

Despite all the changes over the years the firm is still very much a family concern: Like their father, Malcolm Barnsdale's sons, Jason and Matthew, are now both qualified Chartered Surveyors and may well add a fourth generation to the family business. In the meantime the firm of C Barnsdale & Son is both proud of its past and looking forward to an exciting future in its second century.

£1,000. House prices, which today are a permanent topic of conversation in every pub and cafe, had yet to assume the critical importance in our lives which they would soon become.

Many of those who bought their first homes in the 1960s and 1970s would bless Barnsdale & Son when in future years they saw the value of their property soar to levels which they could never have imagined. Many of those who continued renting were now inspired to go out and buy - and often through Barnsdale & Son in the knowledge that they were dealing with an estate agent whose reputation for helpfulness was unrivalled.

In the early 1970s Malcolm's brother Frederick, usually known as 'Butch' Barnsdale helping to distinguish him from his father, joined the firm and became responsible for the residential management whilst Malcolm concentrated on residential sales, valuations and surveys.

The commercial property department also expanded and Neal Craven was appointed Partner in charge of that department in 1991.

Expansion continued with the acquisition of North's Estate agency of Hatfield and Thorne, and although the Hatfield office closed down when the lease expired the Thorne office continues to flourish.

Above left: *Charles Barnsdale & Son offices in the 1970s.* *Above right:* *F G Barnsdale, son of the founder and father of Malcolm and Butch Barnsdale.* *Below:* *Partners of firm (from left to right): Malcolm Barnsdale, Paul Wildsmith, Butch Barnsdale and Neil Craven pictured in 2003 when Paul Wildsmith was appointed a Partner.*

The (im)print of the past

'What good are thousands of copies of books when so few folk know how to read?' was a question some pessimist must inevitably have asked Thomas Caxton when he introduced the printing press to England in 1476. In theory the demand for printed works of all kinds from books to advertising leaflets should have been small in a world where the literate formed just a small minority of the population: in reality the demand for the printed word was, and remains, insatiable.

Doncaster's own successor to Thomas Caxton is Askew Design & Print. The family firm may not be able to trace its origins back to the 15th century, but it certainly goes back far longer than most.

In 1922 George William Askew, no doubt buoyed up with misplaced optimism in the short-lived post war economic boom which followed the ending of the first world war in 1918, established his own printing business in the Doncaster Market Place. George had earlier served his apprenticeship with Alfred King & Sons Scholastic Printers of Oundle, where he had begun work in 1901. The Doncaster family business would still be being run by George's descendants in the 21st century.

Though orphaned at birth George Askew had as a result inherited a considerable sum of money; he lived with an Aunt who sent him to Oundle School. Young George's future life should have been easy but disaster was waiting in the wings: a solicitor embezzled all of his funds and fled to Australia,

leaving the unlucky youngster minus his inheritance and making an apprenticeship a necessity.

George was joined in his printing business by his son Gordon Askew in 1927. On the outbreak of war in 1939 Gordon joined the 1st Derbyshire Yeomanry seeing active service in North Africa, Italy France and Germany. It was however business as usual back in Doncaster: whilst Gordon was away fighting for King and country his wife Constance kept the presses turning in his absence. Gordon finally took over the business from his father in 1953 and immediately began looking for new premises.

One of Gordon's favourite expressions was 'They found it couldn't be done, so they set to with a smile - and still found it couldn't be done'. The search for new premises proved futile. Eventually however a site at High Fishergate did become available - but not until 1966. The fine new building was entered in the Civic Trust competition for 'Constructions

Above: George William Askew, founder of the business, pictured outside his Doncaster Market Place premises in 1935. **Below left:** Askew's High Fishergate site, 1960s. **Below:** Maurice Askew (left) and his father Gordon at High Fishergate.

of computers and automated machinery, which remarkably have simultaneously both improved quality and cut prices.

A new building in Heaven's Walk, still the Askew base, was able to accommodate the firm's 18 staff and also provided plenty of car parking space and offered easy access to the motorway network. Even the large new building would however eventually prove inadequate, and phase one of a planned expansion was completed in 2000 when a pre-press studio was built. A second extension was completed in 2002.

Today the company, now trading as Askew Design & Print is run by the last of the Askew line, James Askew, the great grandson of the firm's founder.

Meanwhile even more investment in hi-tech high speed equipment is already underway: as Gordon Askew was fond of saying 'The race is never won'!

of Architectural merit' it had been designed so that its lines were made to mould into the background, and to complement the grand St George's Church nearby.

It was in the early 1960s that Gordon had introduced the now well-known, and most-used, Helvetica typeface, he was the first printer in the country to do so. Gordon's innovations would ensure the form's continuing growth and appeal to clients

It wasn't long before an extension was needed as business developed and grew. Another extension was added to the High Fishergate building in the late 1980s.

In 1993 however a compulsory purchase order meant that Askew Printers were on the move yet again.

By this time Gordon's son Maurice Askew was at the helm - although Gordon would remain active in the business until 1995.

Maurice would witness enormous changes in printing over his working life as printing methods changed radically in the later decades of the 20th century with the introduction

Top left: Askew's staff photograph, 1992.
Below: Maurice Askew congratulates his son and fourth generation of the Askew family, James, as he takes the helm at Askew Design & Print.
Bottom: Askew Design & Print Heaven's Walk site pictured after extension work in February 2000.

Hot ices

In the Summer of 2000 the one thing Doncaster folk would have liked was a nice cool ice cream. Members of the fire brigade who attended a blaze in Doncaster's Church Street would have liked nothing better than an ice-cream too. Fire-fighters from Doncaster, Adwick and Edlington who tackled the fire, which took two hours to get under control, got their ice creams. Sadly their treat was only in melted form as the flames raced through Allied Massarella's - these days better known as Ice Cream Direct's - cash and carry depot.

One thing we all remember from our childhood is the taste of ice-cream. The story of ice-cream goes back a very long way indeed. According to legend the first Englishman to sample ice-cream was King Richard the Lionheart whose remarkably chivalrous opponent during the Crusades was Saladin: during one scorching 12th century Summer in the Holy Land Saladin is said to have sent Richard Coeur de Lyon ice-cream made using ice brought by relays of riders racing from far away mountain tops.

The trick of bringing ice from distant mountain peaks still snowy in June and July was said to have been practised even earlier by the Roman Emperors. In the 19th century, in a distant homage to the luxurious lives of the long-gone Caesars, ice-cream making once more became something of an Italian speciality. But now the development of commercial ice-making equipment meant that for the first time ice could be produced in large enough quantities to make everyone happy. Not surprisingly because of Italy's sunny weather Italians simply lapped up ice-cream - and what is more they began expanding production and sales throughout Europe, not least to the shores of Britain where they launched a new Roman conquest.

Italian ice-cream vendors riding tricycles with insulated boxes filled with ice creams would became a familiar sight on Britain's streets. The very oldest residents of our town may still just remember the Hokey-pokey man as these ice-cream salesmen where called.

That Italian heritage is still with us today, recalled in such names as 'tutti frutti' the Italian for all fruits, and in a '99' meaning the very best, and named after the 99 hand picked member s of the King of Italy's Royal bodyguard.

The history of Doncaster's Ice Cream Direct began with

Top: *The company's fleet of ice-cream vans in the 1960s.* ***Left:*** *David Dimon, owner of Ice Cream Direct.*

the Massarella family, who were well known as pioneers in ice cream production in England from the 1860s. The Massarellas no longer own the business but have continued in the catering industry, including branching out into farming. The current owner, Dave Dimon, bought the business from Andrew Massarella following his retirement in 1985. Despite a fire in June 2000, which almost destroyed the building, the original Belmont House cash and carry facility in Bentley still stands and carries the old Massarella family name (Allied Massarellas). Although upholding the traditional values of the business, Dave Dimon has moved the company forward to meet the ever-changing demands of the ice-cream industry. The most significant changes being the move away from production and retailing toward wholesale distribution. The company

had a trading alliance with Lyons Maid, now Nestle Ice Cream, which was extended to Treats (Richmond) in 1989. In 1999, after becoming a Walls franchisee in 1991, the company was named as Birds-Eye Walls franchisee Operator of the Year. In line with the demands of the market Ice Cream Direct has since added brands such as Mars and Cadburys to the range of products it supplies.

Operating as Ice Cream Direct, the company distributes ice-cream to an established client base around Yorkshire and Humberside, supplying popular products such as Walls, Treats/Nestle, Mars, Cadbury and Stella. In addition to wholesale distribution, a fleet of ice-cream vans still operate from the Belmont depot covering local areas and events, including popular places of recreation in the local and surrounding areas.

The fire in June 2000 threatened the future of the business, but by 2003, the depot had been fully restored and Ice Cream Direct continued as a leading name in the local distribution of ice cream to a wide range of clients including shops, cafes, theatres and much more.

Left: *The gutted remain of Allied Massarella's ice cream cash and carry in Church Street after the fire in June 2000.* ***Below:*** *Part of the company fleet outside Allied Massarella's ice cream cash and carry.*

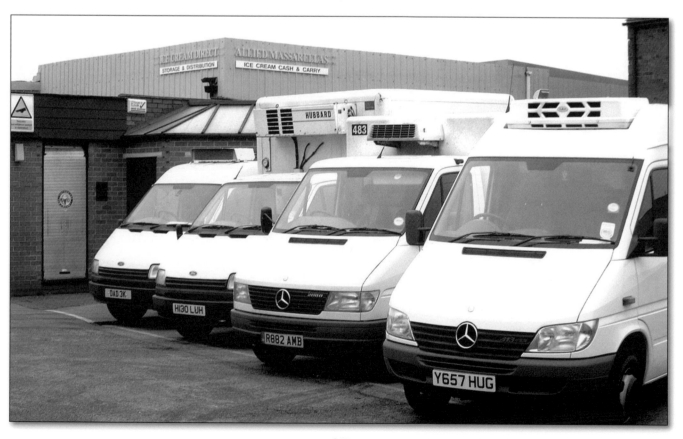

160 years of engineering

One of the most respected names amongst consulting engineers is that of Doncaster's Grantham, Brundell & Farran. The firm has been involved in a vast range of engineering projects from railways to reservoirs.

Since 1958 the firm has been based in Pillar House, South Parade, a building with a long history of its own, having been built in the late 18th century, and in which the Prince of Wales (later George IV) and the Duke of Clarence (later William IV) came to stay in 1806 when attending Doncaster races.

The origins of Grantham, Brundell & Farran however go back 'only' to 1844 when Richard Boxall Grantham set himself up as a consulting engineer in London. His son Richard Fuge Grantham took over on the founder's death in 1891.

Benjamin Shaw Brundell started the Doncaster practice in 1857, on his death in 1897 his nephew, Henry A Brundell, became senior partner. Charles Ernest Farran joined the firm in 1926, becoming senior partner in 1928. The London practice of RB Grantham & Son was acquired in 1935. After the second world war when CE Farran's son TAD Farran rejoined the firm after service in the Far East the two practices were formally amalgamated under the present name.

A native of Norfolk, Benjamin Shaw Brundell specialised in railway construction. In 1857, as major works on the Great

Northern Railway were drawing to a close, Brundell decided to make his home in Doncaster and set up on his own account. One of his first clients was Captain William Peel who commissioned Brundell to design a private railway from Sandy to Potton on his estate - the line ultimately became part of the Oxford to Cambridge railway.

Top left: *Benjamin Shaw Brundell.*
Above: *Harry A Brundell.* ***Below:*** *A 1933 picture of the reconstruction of Sprotbrough Bridge engineered by C E Farran.*

A significant event in 1864 was Brundell's appointment as engineer to the Dun Drainage Commissioners; this was the first work the firm undertook in the field of river engineering and land drainage. In 1869 Brundell took offices at 1 Princes Street where the firm would be based for 89 years.

In 1872, at the request of the Doncaster Corporation, Brundell drew up the plans for a sewerage farm at Sandall and a pumping station at the Holmes - amongst the earliest of their kind.

That same year Brundell also prepared the plans for a reservoir at Thrybergh between Doncaster and Rotherham which would provide clean water for the town's citizens who until then had to use water from the River Don, already polluted by sewerage from Rotherham and Sheffield. The work included an underground aqueduct 10 miles long and was opened in October 1880.

Between 1908 and 1911 Phillip Brundell (HA Brundell's brother) was responsible for the complete planning, layout and design of the new Bentley Colliery Village. From 1912 onwards the firm also became closely involved in negotiations between the various local land drainage authorities and colliery owners over measures to protect low lying areas around Doncaster from subsidence.

On HA Brundell's death in 1928 Charles E Farran was appointed Engineer to the Dun Drainage Commissioners in his place.

The decades which followed would see a steady increase in activity such as the construction of a new pumping station in 1940 to drain land adjoining the left bank of the Don between Doncaster and Thorne - possibly the last steam powered pump ever installed.

Twenty years later in the lower Don Valley the firm would be increasing the capacity of Kirk Bramwith pumping station by 50 per cent with the construction of an extension to receive a three foot diameter diesel-driven pump.

Meanwhile developing farming policy led to grants becoming available for irrigation installations, and the firm designed several schemes including the provision of reservoirs.

In the 1980s the firm would steadily increase its client base and range of expertise, setting up a separate structural engineering department in 1988. The firm would become responsible for an ever increasing number of land drainage pumping stations, the majority of which had originally been designed by them. By the mid 1990s more than 100 such stations were being maintained and operated by them.

Today, with equal skill and dedication, the firm's modern day partners Bruce Gelsthorpe, Riley South and Jennifer Clark continue to add to the astonishing legacy of works bequeathed to us by their professional forbears.

Top: *Charles Ernest Farran (top) and T A D (Ted) Farran.* ***Above left:*** *The firms premises, Pillar House, Doncaster. Harry A Brundell.* ***Left:*** *Partners (from left to right) Riley South, Bruce Gelsthorpe and Jennifer Clark.*

Wood you believe it?

The joinery products of Jeld-Wen UK Ltd, a company located on the north side of Doncaster's Watch House Lane, are distributed throughout the UK to builders' merchants, leading house builders and to local authorities which use, stock and sell the firm's John Carr and Boulton & Paul brands.

Based in Oregon in the USA the Jeld-Wen group of companies started out as a small millwork plant in 1960. Today with more than 20,000 employees world-wide the company is one of the leading manufacturers of windows, doors and other related joinery products in the world. The Jeld-Wen name first appeared in Doncaster only in 1999, though the local name which it had acquired, that of the late John Carr, had a history in the town going back to the early 1930s.

The South Yorkshire Woodworking Company had been founded by a local builder Frank Haslam in 1933. In 1939 30-year old John Carr bought the company, then based on the south side of Watch House Lane.

During the war years all production was dedicated to the war effort, and output included rifle boxes, packing cases for Spitfires and Wellington bombers, Bailey Bridges and wooden accommodation units. Over 600 people were employed during this period working round the clock in shifts. In the early 1940s John Carr bought around 30 acres of land on the north side of Watch House Lane; he earmarked the land for future expansion.

Top: The original joiners shop at Doncaster.
Below: A Doncaster mill in the 1930s.

factory was built at Corby in 1982. In the 1980s other companies, Sharpe Brothers and Knight Ltd of Burton on Trent, Rothervale Joinery and later Allan Bros of Berwick on Tweed, were acquired.

The Doncaster head office of what was now a group of companies was enlarged several times to accommodate growing staff numbers. In 1985 the business was merged with the Rugby Group Plc renowned for its Rugby Cement operations. Founder John Carr retired from business on his 80th birthday in 1989.

There followed a series of small acquisitions by the Rugby Group followed in February 1997 by the purchase of the leading player in the UK joinery industry, Boulton & Paul Ltd, a firm with roots going back to 18th century Norwich ironmongers but which had moved into windows, doors and kitchens after the second world war.

At the end of the war there was an acute shortage of housing, a shortage which provided an opportunity for rapid growth of the business, even though the supply of imported timber would remain uncertain for some years.

In 1945 a flush door factory was set up in Rotherham; later stair cases too would be produced there. Another factory was established at Witham in Essex for the manufacture of wooden surrounds for Crittal Steel Windows.

The company was floated on the London Stock Exchange in 1954. The continuity of the Carr family involvement was assured when Peter Carr joined his father in the business in 1960.

Peter Carr would in due course become joint Managing Director with John S Woolley who had been Company Secretary since 1947. John Woolley had been one of the team that looked after the business when John Carr had contracted polio in 1947 - an illness which left him unable to walk without the aid of leg callipers and sticks. In 1961 John Woolley's son Roger also joined the company as timber yard manager, eventually becoming a company director himself.

Amalgamation later in 1997 saw the formation of Rugby Joinery UK Ltd.

In the summer of 1999 Jeld-Wen invested in the UK, buying Rugby Joinery Ltd from the Rugby Group. The Rugby Joinery name was relinquished, though the leading name in doors, windows and stairs John Carr and Boulton & Paul were retained as product brands of Jeld-Wen.

Top left: *Pre 1944 photograph of the window shop site.*
Left: *The reception area at Jeld-Wen UK Ltd.*
Below: *The company premises in Watch House Lane, Doncaster.*

With the exception of doors all the company's products were made to measure: it was only in the late 1960s that a standard joinery catalogue would be introduced.

A factory would open on Gloucester in 1963. The Rotherham works closed in 1970 and a state-of-the -art flush door factory was built in Doncaster. A timber frame

Acknowledgments

The publishers would like to thank

Doncaster Library & Information Services

Liz Appleyard

Ray Atkin

E Bell

A J Custons

Geoff Elvin

Gordon Evans

David Jamson

Ralph Mann

Derek Porter

Kate Pounder

E M Walter

Dawn White

Andrew Mitchell

Steve Ainsworth

True North Books Ltd - Book List

Memories of Accrington - 1 903204 05 4

Memories of Barnet - 1 903204 16 X

Memories of Barnsley - 1 900463 11 3

Golden Years of Barnsley -1 900463 87 3

Memories of Basingstoke - 1 903204 26 7

Memories of Bedford - 1 900463 83 0

More Memories of Bedford - 1 903204 33 X

Golden Years of Birmingham - 1 900463 04 0

Birmingham Memories - 1 903204 45 3

Memories of Blackburn - 1 900463 40 7

More Memories of Blackburn - 1 900463 96 2

Memories of Blackpool - 1 900463 21 0

Memories of Bolton - 1 900463 45 8

More Memories of Bolton - 1 900463 13 X

Bolton Memories - 1 903204 37 2

Memories of Bournemouth -1 900463 44 X

Memories of Bradford - 1 900463 00 8

More Memories of Bradford - 1 900463 16 4

More Memories of Bradford II - 1 900463 63 6

Bradford Memories - 1 903204 47 X

Bradford City Memories - 1 900463 57 1

Memories of Bristol - 1 900463 78 4

More Memories of Bristol - 1 903204 43 7

Memories of Bromley - 1 903204 21 6

Memories of Burnley - 1 900463 95 4

Golden Years of Burnley - 1 900463 67 9

Memories of Bury - 1 900463 90 3

Memories of Cambridge - 1 900463 88 1

Memories of Cardiff - 1 900463 14 8

More Memories of Cardiff - 1 903204 73 9

Memories of Carlisle - 1 900463 38 5

Memories of Chelmsford - 1 903204 29 1

Memories of Cheltenham - 1 903204 17 8

Memories of Chester - 1 900463 46 6

More Memories of Chester -1 903204 02 X

Memories of Chesterfield -1 900463 61 X

More Memories of Chesterfield - 1 903204 28 3

Memories of Colchester - 1 900463 74 1

Nostalgic Coventry - 1 900463 58 X

Coventry Memories - 1 903204 38 0

Memories of Croydon - 1 900463 19 9

More Memories of Croydon - 1 903204 35 6

Golden Years of Darlington - 1 900463 72 5

Nostalgic Darlington - 1 900463 31 8

Darlington Memories - 1 903204 46 1

Memories of Derby - 1 900463 37 7

More Memories of Derby - 1 903204 20 8

Memories of Dewsbury & Batley - 1 900463 80 6

Memories of Doncaster - 1 900463 36 9

More Memories of Doncaster - 1 903204 75 5

Nostalgic Dudley - 1 900463 03 2

Golden Years of Dudley - 1 903204 60 7

Memories of Edinburgh - 1 900463 33 4

More memories of Edinburgh - 1903204 72 0

Memories of Enfield - 1 903204 14 3

Memories of Exeter - 1 900463 94 6

Memories of Glasgow - 1 900463 68 7

More Memories of Glasgow - 1 903204 44 5

Memories of Gloucester - 1 903204 04 6

Memories of Grimsby - 1 900463 97 0

More Memories of Grimsby - 1 903204 36 4

Memories of Guildford - 1 903204 22 4

Memories of Halifax - 1 900463 05 9

More Memories of Halifax - 1 900463 06 7

Golden Years of Halifax - 1 900463 62 8

Nostalgic Halifax - 1 903204 30 5

Memories of Harrogate - 1 903204 01 1

Memories of Hartlepool - 1 900463 42 3

Memories of High Wycombe - 1 900463 84 9

Memories of Huddersfield - 1 900463 15 6

More Memories of Huddersfield - 1 900463 26 1

Golden Years of Huddersfield - 1 900463 77 6

Nostalgic Huddersfield - 1 903204 19 4

Huddersfield Town FC - 1 900463 51 2

Memories of Hull - 1 900463 86 5

More Memories of Hull - 1 903204 06 2

Hull Memories - 1 903204 70 4

Memories of Ipswich - 1 900463 09 1

More Memories of Ipswich - 1 903204 52 6

Memories of Keighley - 1 900463 01 6

Golden Years of Keighley - 1 900463 92 X

True North Books Ltd - Book List

Memories of Kingston - 1 903204 24 0

Memories of Leeds - 1 900463 75 X

More Memories of Leeds - 1 900463 12 1

Golden Years of Leeds - 1 903204 07 0

Memories of Leicester - 1 900463 08 3

Leeds Memories - 1 903204 62 3

More Memories of Leicester - 1 903204 08 9

Memories of Leigh - 1 903204 27 5

Memories of Lincoln - 1 900463 43 1

Memories of Liverpool - 1 900463 07 5

More Memories of Liverpool - 1 903204 09 7

Liverpool Memories - 1 903204 53 4

Memories of Luton - 1 900463 93 8

Memories of Macclesfield - 1 900463 28 8

Memories of Manchester - 1 900463 27 X

More Memories of Manchester - 1 903204 03 8

Manchester Memories - 1 903204 54 2

Memories of Middlesbrough - 1 900463 56 3

More Memories of Middlesbrough - 1 903204 42 9

Memories of Newbury - 1 900463 79 2

Memories of Newcastle - 1 900463 81 4

More Memories of Newcastle - 1 903204 10 0

Newcastle Memories - 1.903204 71 2

Memories of Newport - 1 900463 59 8

Memories of Northampton - 1 900463 48 2

More Memories of Northampton - 1 903204 34 8

Memories of Norwich - 1 900463 73 3

Memories of Nottingham - 1 900463 91 1

More Memories of Nottingham - 1 903204 11 9

Nottingham Memories - 1 903204 63 1

Bygone Oldham - 1 900463 25 3

Memories of Oldham - 1 900463 76 8

Memories of Oxford - 1 900463 54 7

Memories of Peterborough - 1 900463 98 9

Golden Years of Poole - 1 900463 69 5

Memories of Portsmouth - 1 900463 39 3

More Memories of Portsmouth - 1 903204 51 8

Nostalgic Preston - 1 900463 50 4

More Memories of Preston - 1 900463 17 2

Preston Memories - 1 903204 41 0

Memories of Reading - 1 900463 49 0

Memories of Rochdale - 1 900463 60 1

More Memories of Reading - 1 903204 39 9

More Memories of Rochdale - 1 900463 22 9

Memories of Romford - 1 903204 40 2

Memories of St Albans - 1 903204 23 2

Memories of St Helens - 1 900463 52 0

Memories of Sheffield - 1 900463 20 2

More Memories of Sheffield - 1 900463 32 6

Golden Years of Sheffield - 1 903204 13 5

Memories of Slough - 1 900 463 29 6

Golden Years of Solihull - 1 903204 55 0

Memories of Southampton - 1 900463 34 2

More Memories of Southampton - 1 903204 49 6

Memories of Stockport - 1 900463 55 5

More Memories of Stockport - 1 903204 18 6

Memories of Stockton - 1 900463 41 5

Memories of Stoke-on-Trent - 1 900463 47 4

More Memories of Stoke-on-Trent - 1 903204 12 7

Memories of Stourbridge - 1903204 31 3

Memories of Sunderland - 1 900463 71 7

More Memories of Sunderland - 1 903204 48 8

Memories of Swindon - 1 903204 00 3

Memories of Uxbridge - 1 900463 64 4

Memories of Wakefield - 1 900463 65 2

More Memories of Wakefield - 1 900463 89 X

Nostalgic Walsall - 1 900463 18 0

Golden Years of Walsall - 1 903204 56 9

More Memories of Warrington - 1 900463 02 4

Memories of Watford - 1 900463 24 5

Golden Years of West Bromwich - 1 900463 99 7

Memories of Wigan - 1 900463 85 7

Golden Years of Wigan - 1 900463 82 2

Nostalgic Wirral - 1 903204 15 1

Wirral Memories - 1 903204 747

Memories of Woking - 1 903204 32 1

Nostalgic Wolverhampton - 1 900463 53 9

Wolverhampton Memories - 1 903204 50 X

Memories of Worcester - 1 903204 25 9

Memories of Wrexham - 1 900463 23 7

Memories of York - 1 900463 66 0

Available in the Local Interest section of all major bookshops or direct from the publishers - telephone 01422 344344